TwoTankersDown

Robert Frump

The Greatest Small-Boat Rescue
in U.S. Coast Guard History

THE LYONS PRESS
Guilford, Connecticut
An imprint of The Globe Pequot Press

The Lyons Press is an imprint of The Globe Pequot Press.

Unless otherwise noted, all photos are courtesy of the U.S. Coast Guard.

Text design by Kim Burdick

Library of Congress Cataloging-in-Publication Data is available on file.

ISBN 978-1-59921-337-8

Printed in the United States of America

10 9 8 7 6 5 4 3 2 1

For Sarah
Who is brave and wise.

"*The Coast Guard is always at war; against all enemies of mankind at sea: fire, collision, lawlessness, gales, derelicts and many more. The Coast Guard, therefore, is no place for a quitter or for a crybaby, or for a four-flusher, or for anyone who cannot 'keep their eye on the ball'....*"

—Letter of Enlistment Acceptance sent to
Bernard C. Webber, 1946

↩

Colonel Gates: *You're scared, right?*
Private *Vig: Maybe.*
Gates: *The way it works is, you do the thing you're scared … of, and you get the courage after you do it, not before you do it.*
Vig: *That's a dumb… way to work. It should be the other way around.*
Gates: *I know. That's the way it works.*

—Dialogue, *from Three Kings*

Contents

CONTENTS

Preface

This is a work of nonfiction written in the form of a story. The *Pendleton* rescue has been written about before from the standpoint of the rescue crew. To my knowledge, no other book exists that tells the story of both the *Fort Mercer* and *Pendleton* rescues from the viewpoint of both those on the tankers and the rescuers. The *Fort Mercer* story in particular deserves an at-length treatment, as aspects of it were every bit as incredible as the *Pendleton's*.

The genesis of this book began with my first maritime book, *Until the Sea Shall Free Them*, about the wreck of the SS *Marine Electric* in 1983. My editors at the time suggested that my long description of the *Pendleton* rescue was too much of a detour from the voyage of the *Marine Electric* story and deserved its own book. My hope is that they were correct.

I prefer a narrative approach to nonfiction because the telling of a story presents facts in an accessible manner within a context of nuance and emotion. Observations, conclusions, interpretations, nuance, and opinion in this form of writing belong to the narrator-writer and fairly so, I feel, if that disclosure between writer and reader is fully made.

This does not give the writer license to mint fact. I've attempted to address concerns about fact here through the inclusion of source notes and bibliography at the end of the book. This alone is no antidote to the misuse of facts or their use out of context, but it is my hope they send a signal of purpose: I do not take facts lightly, nor do I knowingly misrepresent them. As the late Patrick Moynihan once said, "Everyone is entitled to his own opinion, but not his own facts." You will find opinion and interpretation here, but the facts are, well, the facts.

So there are no compound characters, no hypothetical scenes presented as real. This story is not "fact-based" or "inspired by true events." To the best of my ability, I've written a story that I believe presents the facts of the situation and, with luck, some truths as well. The drama of these rescues stands on its own with no need of embellishment or exaggeration.

One

TANKER MEN

February 12, 1952
Baton Rouge and Norco, Louisiana
Aboard the SS *Pendleton* and the SS *Fort Mercer*

The big tanker, nearly the size of two football fields stretched end-to-end lay at dockside, half-filled with 15,000 tons of heating oil and kerosene. A slender stem of pipe and hose ran from her deck across a narrow slice of the Lower Mississippi River Basin and disappeared into a whole huge farm of silos and storage tanks in the Louisiana bayou country near Baton Rouge. It was through this straw that the SS *Pendleton*, 503 feet stem to stern, seemed to sip, feed, and sink, like a huge swollen tick, lower and lower into the water on a warm, summerlike night, February 12, 1952.

This was a time when any tanker captain got the jitters. Nervous little thoughts and fears bumped and sizzled the consciousness like the bugs buzzing about and banging into the lines of lights that lit the tanker decks. Captain John Fitzgerald of the *Pendleton* was not an exception. He had been through the war and seen it all. Yet seven years after the fighting stopped, any good tanker captain remained alert at a wartime level when the tankers were neither full nor empty.

1

There was good reason to be nervous. Fumes filled the big tanks of the tanker and mixed with oxygen. When the mixture of oil and air reached a certain critical point, it could explode. Even Daniel Ludwig, now the multi-millionaire owner of fleets of tankers, found out what could happen back in 1926 when he was a young captain in Boston on the tanker *Phoenix*.

He heard his crew calling for help from below. Fumes were overwhelming them. Ludwig rushed to the rescue and pounded down the ladder into the hold after them.

Later, they figured the nails in his boots produced a spark on the steel ladder. For the men below, it was like a bomb. The crew died instantly. For Ludwig, with his hands still on the ladder, the blast was like a rocket engine. He was propelled out of the hold, up the ladder, and into the air in an arc and landed 25 feet away.

Now, in 1952, Daniel Ludwig was the father of the supertanker and well onto being the richest man in the world. And the same problems still pained him, literally. Severe pain in his back from that explosion would accompany him the rest of his life. And on a larger scale, regarding the larger pain, platoons of Ludwig scientists and engineers never could wholly solve the problem of explosions. Tankers could be bombs. The smallest source of energy could spark the fuse.

So Captain Fitzgerald kept a close watch over the ship as she was loaded, and so did his chief mate, Martin Moe. It was close to eighty degrees in Baton Rouge, and Moe, in charge of loading, could see the wafts of the fumes of the cargo; he could smell them, too. Kerosene had a light, sharper odor to it that could sting your nose. The heating oil had a danker smell, a bass note on the olfactory scale. Some inevitably spilled into the water and formed greasy rainbows. Fumes from both cargoes intermingled and provided a chemical-infused micro-atmosphere, a bit like the service bay of an auto mechanic's garage. It was muggy. Close.

Raymond Sybert was the chief engineer of the ship, and any engineer had to love the SS *Pendleton* and the modern miracle this ship was. The explosion problem was not solved, but technology had eased it. She was welded, for one thing. Ludwig always hated the old riveted ships and felt the explosion that hurt him was caused in part by leaks of fumes flowing through loose rivet fits. Welded ships did not leak—at least not like the riveted ships did.

In the old days, too, loading tankers involved laborious measurements in a series of tanks, each separately serviced from the outside. Load one tank to full and keep the others light and the ship could be dangerously out of balance. Fumes, sparks, cigarettes, cutting torches, oxygen all could come together disastrously. Tanks billowed wavy lines of gases to the deck. A dropped set of car keys, a careless welder: anything could set it off.

But on the *Pendleton*, Moe and Sybert could pump and dump oil wherever they wanted it. They could fill tank 1 and without much of a pause switch the incoming flow of oil to tank number 2. Or if the tanks already filled needed trimming, Moe could pump oil from tank number 5 to tank 2 and from there to 3, if he so chose. If the ship was 6 inches lower at the stern than it was at the bow, he could pump cargo forward and trim the ship. All of this was in a closed circuit, more or less, with far fewer fumes wafting anywhere more than they had to.

And below? In the engine room? It was an electrical engineer's dream. They had built these tankers during the war and designated them T-2s. Like most ships of the time, the T-2s relied on steam power. But unlike other ships, the steam did not directly turn turbines that turned the prop. On T-2s, the steam turned turbines that produced electricity, and the electricity drove huge electric engines.

The design was that rarest of commodities: a luxury born of necessity. Reduction gears used in conventional turbine drives were in short supply during the war, and the electrical engines were an elegant workaround. The even pull, the control, the smoothness Sybert could employ using these engines was extraordinary. He could move from full ahead to full astern if he wanted to. The T-2s were great wartime ships. When

German bombers were reported en route to a port, the captains of regular ships needed to build up steam. The T-2 captains just put it in drive and did an electro-glide out of harm's way.

And the power? It was no exaggeration. It was no metaphor. T-2s had been used often in the post-war period in third world countries. The ships would dock and thick cords would be snaked ashore. The ships literally lit whole cities.

Now, post war, there were hundreds of them out there. And this was their coast—the tanker coast of Louisiana and Texas. America was booming and all along the Gulf, the T-2s were tied up to docks outside tank farms and refineries and their long slender hoses and pipes sucked in oil. They would feed and when filled cast off and head to the Northeast coast.

Not far from the *Pendleton*, downriver at Norco, Louisiana, very close to New Orleans, the SS *Fort Mercer*, another T-2, was also taking on a cargo of heating oil and kerosene from the big Shell Oil facility there.

They were nearly identical ships with just a few differences. The *Pendleton* was bound for Boston and carried more heating oil than kerosene. The *Fort Mercer* was heading slightly north of there to Portland in Maine and carried more kerosene than heating oil.

Also, the *Fort Mercer* loaded slightly light. On a normal trip, she would have exited Norco through Southwest Pass, but a ship was stranded there. So she needed to take an alternate route, a shallower route. She could not carry her normal full load because she would not clear the new passage. So she loaded light—30 feet forward and 30 feet aft in fresh water—with the forward deep tanks essentially empty. Once she hit the salt water, her draft would rise slightly to about 29.5 feet. The *Pendleton* loaded about 1 foot deeper in fresh and salt water.

Aside from that, they were the same ship. They were 503 feet long and about 70 feet wide. Each produced around 6,600 horsepower. They both had nine cargo tanks. And they both departed on the same day: February 12.

At the helm of the *Fort Mercer*, Captain Frederick Paetzel had the hardened nerves of a wartime merchant officer. He was a large man, a bit overweight, and some of the crew thought him too harsh an officer, though this was by no means universally shared. Some did not know him, nor he them. The vessels each carried a crew of more than forty: forty-three for the *Fort Mercer*; forty-seven for the *Pendleton*. Men came, men went.

Willard Fahrner, the second mate, thought Paetzel was just fine. Fine enough anyway, a steady guy. Fahrner, like most of the other men, was happy to be in the coastal trades where they made runs to Boston or Maine, six days up and six days back. America was booming and the dreams put on hold by the war for men like Fahrner were now coming true.

There was a time and place he dreamed of little but surviving, after all: June 23, 1943, the tanker *Stamvac Manilla*, in the southwest Pacific, not far from New Guinea. A Japanese torpedo had split the ship Fahrner served on and he knew what true danger at sea could be. Merchant mariners, man-for-man, had suffered more war casualties than any branch of the service except the Marines.

But this duty? Well, tankers had their troubles. But the coastal run was a piece of cake. You did it so many times you could do it in your sleep.

So when the ships headed to sea, they both followed a common route: down the dredged-out channel of the Lower Mississippi, across the well-worn sea-lanes of the Gulf of Mexico, around Florida and up the Eastern Seaboard. The bridge and officer quarters of both ships were located forward, atop a small housing that ran up three stories from the deck, a bit more than a third of the ship's length back from the bow. The engineers and crew stayed aft in a larger housing near the stern of the ship. A narrow, railed catwalk connected the two command centers.

All those things the two ships had in common one with each other: design, cargo, configuration, and destination. And then there was the other thing, too—the thing all T-2s seemed to share, the part the men knew at some level but did not talk much about. These ships were built in wartime. They had done their job. But the builders had been rushed. They had used that new welding technology.

How could you say it? Some of the ships weren't solid. But you didn't know which ones, really. The Coast Guard and the American Bureau of Shipping had acknowledged the problem and required that the ships be reinforced. On the decks of both ships, and below as well, ran thick steel belts, or "crack arrestors."

The crack arrestors were a response to a question that no one had the answer to: What made the ships crack in the first place? Why were some fine and others catastrophes? All the inspectors really knew is that the ships cracked and the big metal bands might help stop the ships from splitting clean in two.

The men walked over these crack arrestors on the deck daily and had to be reminded by the thick riveted belts that there were some structural questions about the ships. But at another level, even those who were skittish did not spend a lot of time worrying about it. Risk was a given. There were so many war stories out there, you'd go crazy thinking about them all.

Besides, there were stories, too, on how tough a ship those T-2s were. How about the SS *Ohio*? She'd left the River Clyde, Scotland, on August 8, 1942, for Malta, carrying 13,000 tons of kerosene and fuel oil desperately needed by the Allies.

Malta was an island where the Allies staged air raids on the Axis ships out of Italy supplying Rommel's tanks in North Africa. Germany was close to taking Alexandria when Axis supplies ran low. Rommel ran out of diesel fuel for his tanks, and the war at this point boiled down to whether Germany could or could not resupply him via its own tankers sailing across the Mediterranean. The Allied bombers and fighters on Malta kept the supply line closed and shut the door on supplies to Rommel.

But then the Allies ran out of gas on Malta. Only the SS *Ohio* could deliver the goods—the gas—in time.

The Junker 88s and Stuka dive-bombers caught up with her on August 11 near North Africa and for three days she was strafed and bombed. An

Italian submarine torpedoed her. Two Junker bombers crashed into her. She lost her rudder, and holes in her hull meant she had only 30 inches of freeboard—less than a yardstick separating her deck from the water. Still, she made it, propped up on either side by destroyers, like two buddies aiding a drunken third. The Allies refueled their planes and kept the door shut on Rommel.

So you could be selective about the truth you wanted to hear: T-2, unsafe at any speed; T-2, indestructible war horse, the ship that may have saved the Allies from defeat in North Africa.

And besides, many of the crew and officers were war veterans who discounted risk at a steep rate. Hell, an assistant cook on the *Fort Mercer* had been a combat marine. They sailed aboard ships that were bombs— and they did this willingly.

Ask them if they were worried about the ship splitting in two at sea and survival in cold waters?

It was a trick question.

They were *tanker men.* It was the explosion that was going to kill them.

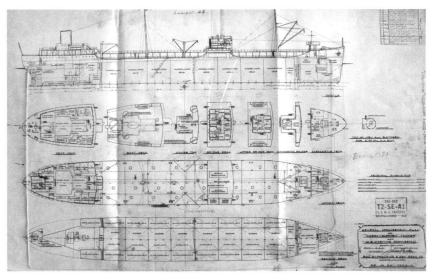

Schematic drawing of a T-2 oil tanker.

Two

THE LIFESAVERS

February 16, 1952
Chatham Lifeboat Station, Chatham Massachusetts

At the Coast Guard Lifeboat Station in Chatham on Cape Cod in Massachusetts, the men had settled into a winter routine. The summer crowd and the calls for sailboat and surf swimmer rescues were long gone. Almost all the jobs now were related to commercial fishing vessels or maintaining navigation aids, and most of those were run-of-the-mill. This boat had broken loose from its moorings. That one was trapped by ice in the harbor. A channel buoy was ripped loose by a storm surge. The lighthouse boat needed provisions.

Bernard C. Webber, a young lifeboat coxswain, had some slack time. He decided the new guys in command were growing on him, but he still dearly missed Frank Masachi and Alvin E. Newcomb, the old commander.

Masachi had saved Webber—not physically, not literally as in a water rescue. But if it had not been for Masachi and the discipline of the Coast Guard, Webber did not know where he would be. A kid in trouble was his guess.

Webber seemed to be someone who did not easily get the hang of things by himself. He needed rules. He needed things clear. He had been in trouble at age fifteen in 1943 in Boston, and it might have been a little thing had it not been for one very big thing. He was the son of a Protestant minister. The trouble was nothing that serious. He would acknowledge that he had been "easily led" by friends. That much he would say and no more.

Was it joyriding? A little drinking? Some close to him at that time said it was nothing that serious—just breaking a few street lights with rocks or rolling about in hedges until they broke. Pretty harmless Huck Finn stuff but a big deal when you were the son of a preacher man. Bigger stuff still when you hung with the Catholics in town, as Bernie did, and the lights and hedges were in the Protestant neighborhoods served by the Tremont Temple Baptist Church, where your father was associate pastor. Worse still when you were undiplomatic enough to get caught.

Mostly, he and Stephen Holden, the kid down the block, were high on the war. It was intoxicating to young teenagers and the adrenaline and the testosterone just could not be contained within wholly acceptable borders. Good lord, the country was at war. Friends of theirs just a few years older than they were heroes. Bernie's three older brothers all were in the fray, in the show. You only had to be sixteen to join the merchant marine and already there were stories of glory. So if you could not get into the war, then you got into whatever you could, including trouble.

His father and a well-meaning, well-to-do parishioner had the solution, and it was not sending Bernie to war. Instead, he was sent to a prestigious and expensive boarding school, and he would study for the ministry. His dad knew he was a good kid. Bernie had a good heart. He wanted to help people. He was just very affected by the war. The best schools, the best people would bring out the best in him.

And Webber was holding his own at prep school academically. But he felt out of place. He did not dress like the rich kids. The rich kids worked clearing tables; he worked in the fields and gardens. He'd walk in late to French class smelling like manure and his instructor each time would remind him of that. He did not easily get the hang of things. And this "thing"—an East Coast elite prep school—was something he would never get.

So perhaps it was fate that when his old friend in mischief, Steve Holden, wrecked his father's car, Holden headed straight for Webber. They hid out for a few days in the school. Bernie sneaked food from his dinner to Steve. But it was not long before they got caught. His parents were called but before the Rev. Webber could come and pick him up, Bernie and Steve Holden ran away, plodding through the cornfields outside Northfield, Massachusetts.

Being a fifteen-year-old on the lamb got old quick and Bernie slumped home. There, his father stewed and stewed and then finally relented.

There were programs where sixteen-year-olds could join the merchant marine. Bernie Webber badly wanted to go. He made the case to his dad. Since age twelve, he'd been a Sea Scout, a water-going Boy Scout, with the Wollaston, Massachusetts troop. He loved the sea.

And his dad had to concede the sea was in the family blood. Each summer the Webber family went to a place on the Kennebec River just below Bath, Maine. Bernie's uncles worked at the Bath Iron Works building ships. He was just a small kid when they'd bring him in to watch the big ships being constructed. He'd watch them build the ships and then launch them into the river. Bernie saw those ships moving out to sea, and that's where he wanted to go. His dad *had* to let him go to sea, the young man said.

The Reverend Webber conceded the point. When Bernie turned sixteen, his father signed the papers.

Webber was jubilant. He was on his own and filled with freedom. Bernie even started smoking. It seemed jaunty. Webber was on his way to the war. He joined his first ship in the Panama Canal, cocky as could be. He scrambled up a Jacobs ladder to the deck with a lit cigarette dangling from his mouth ready to take on the world.

The ship was a tanker. The chief mate saw Bernie, saw the cigarette and said nothing. Instead, the chief swung a roundhouse right at Webber that caught him on the cheek and knocked him cold.

Bernie was out for a few minutes. He awoke. The cigarette was gone. The chief mate stood over him and said:

"Did you *learn* anything?"

Webber silently shook his head yes.

"Because if you haven't learned anything, next time I will *personally* throw you over the side," the chief mate said.

The education of Bernie Webber had begun. He spent two years aboard the tanker—a T-2, as it turned out—during wartime, sailing the Caribbean. The ship was fitted out with anti-aircraft cannon and machine guns. But by that time, the Caribbean was quiet, and the ship saw little action, just hours and hours of plowing through the blue-green waters of paradise. These were warm waters. His tanker, the *Sinclair Rubiline*, held up just fine as she ranged from Aruba and Curacao, moving fuel to the South Pacific.

The discipline was good for him, and here, it seemed, he had found the hang of something. When the war was over, he returned to Boston but steered clear of his old habits and friends. He wasn't even eighteen and shipping was a bit slow. You hung out at the union hall and hoped your card would be called. His wasn't. He wondered if he would be drafted into the Army soon if he could not catch a ship, and on a whim one day, at lunchtime when the maritime union office was closed, he wandered over to Constitution Wharf in Boston.

He strolled about and saw a large sign that said, "The Coast Guard Wants You." He was curious and popped into the office. There, a petty officer second class was eating lunch with his feet propped up on his desk. He took one look at young Webber and said, "What the hell do you want?"

Bernie said he'd seen the sign that said the Coast Guard wanted him.

"Well, that doesn't necessarily mean you," the petty officer said.

"I'm a merchant seaman," Webber shot back and the tone shifted there and then. The petty officer prepared papers. Bernie's father needed to sign them as Bernie was still under age, but in the end it all worked and he was accepted.

What he found in the Coast Guard was a hard-core discipline beyond the merchant marine. Right from the beginning, the officers made this clear to the new recruits. "Hard jobs are routine in this service," read his letter of acceptance. "The Coast Guard is always at war; against all enemies of mankind at sea; fire, collision, lawlessness, gales, derelicts and many more. The Coast Guard, therefore, is no place for a quitter or for a crybaby, or for a four-flusher, or for anyone who cannot 'keep their eye on the ball'...."

It was tough, and basic training was the toughest thing Bernie had done. But it worked for him. In fact, it worked better than he could have ever expected.

He had real physical strength. He was 6 foot 2 and you would have called him a big lug if it were not for the fact he was so lean— only about 170 pounds on that frame. And he was smart, too. He'd held his own at the prep school academically. He learned fast. And he had a knack on the

Bernie Webber as a young Coast Guardsman

water for steering, for navigating, for reading the sea and the tides and currents, for knowing where he was when the seas and wind turned most people around.

He liked the idea of a military unit that rescued people, though he was yet to actively achieve that goal.

Once out of basic, he was driven by jeep to Chatham, Massachusetts, on Cape Cod and got a glance at one of the rescue boats as he passed the harbor. It was a strange-looking thing. Stubby with stubborn-looking lines. The boat had no name. CG 36500 was on the vessel in black letters and numerals; that and "Chatham" on the back.

"What's that?" Bernie asked.

"That's a 36-foot rescue boat," the driver said.

The CG 36500 as she appeared when Bernie Webber first saw her in Chatham.
Photo courtesy of the Orleans Historical Society

A Coast Guard photo of a 36-foot lifeboat in heavy seas shows its rugged capabilities.

Webber was unimpressed at first. Soon, though, he noticed just in passing that the rescue boat coxswains—the helmsmen, the wheelmen— carried themselves with what could only be called pride. They were rescuers. There was something to them, an air of substance.

He decided that's what he wanted to do and as he was leaving Chatham, he got another glimpse of the CG 36500. She meant something different this time. He felt a real affection for the boat, as if she were special. He was disappointed when he caught a ride in a 38-foot picket boat, not the 36-footer. He wished it was the CG 36500.

There were whole weeks when he wondered if he would ever ride in a rescue boat. He had spent the first few months of active duty as a seventeen-year-old locked in a lighthouse with a seventy-five-year-old veteran of the old Lifesaving Service. This guy was old line. He would die in the Coast Guard. The old guys never retired.

In fact, Webber was absorbing the culture of the Coast Guard, the social traits that "managed" the agency as much as any rule or regulation. Sometimes for the better, and sometimes for worse. Tradition had it that there was a culture of courage, a small community devoted to this selfless task of rescue. The job paid little except in a currency of the high regard of the community and self-esteem. But the men themselves seemed in some way rich.

There were other traditions, too. Not all of them good. How could you put this? The Coast Guard revered its heroes. But the Coast Guard and the country could forget them as well. For example, the old guy in the lighthouse not too many years ago could not have afforded to retire. Underfunded and forgotten once the romance of rescue faded, the old Lifesaving Service could not pay pensions. Men could not retire.

Toward the end of its life, before the Lifesaving Service merged with the Coast Guard, many of the men who had started as young specimens of the species were rowing toward wrecks in their sixties and seventies, because they had to. Charles McCormack, who won five gold medals for lifesaving and was the most famous of all the old salts, stepped from a lifeboat at age seventy-five, looked toward the sea and said, "Tide is ebbing." Then he dropped dead, leaving his wife and family penniless with no help from the government.

Webber was yet to see that side of the Coast Guard as a young man, and he was benefiting greatly from the good side of the culture. He spent weeks on Monomoy Island, just off Chatham, at a lifeboat station where he had to use rainwater to wash his clothes. It was about as close to the old Lifesaving Service duty as you could get. He paid his dues. And finally, within a year, he moved on to work the motorized lifeboats.

They just seemed to grow on him as he understood more about them and how to run them, and once he did, he could not remember why he ever thought them odd-looking. They were crafts of extraordinary grace and beauty, he believed, blessed with great design and function.

At the start, though, he knew little. Masachi drilled him and drilled him, tested and retested, sent the seventeen-year-old on hours of endless patrols. Now, where he was six years later, seemed perfect: the Chatham Coast Guard Lifeboat Station at the elbow of Cape Cod in Massachusetts. Webber thought it the most beautiful and charmed place on Earth. It was blessed with harbors and a town that looked like a post card. The Coast Guard unit itself was contained within its own small culture, almost like the old U.S. Lifesaving Service with its surf men who would live for weeks and weeks in isolated stretches of wild beach land.

Yet, the station was also a part of the town. The men would be ten days on and two days off in the lifeboat station, but not all of that was in isolation. They would patrol the harbor and help the local fishermen secure astray boats. And it was not uncommon for them to aid in a rescue, particularly near the notorious Chatham Bar where the big Atlantic rollers met shallower water.

Fishing vessels had to cross the Chatham Bar to reach the Atlantic. In foul weather it was impassable—a thunderous churning of white water on shallow sand. Even in fair weather, it was dicey. Frequently the returning boats, loaded with fish, would be pitch-poled, turned over and over, by the big rollers coming from behind. Webber and the other Coast-guardsmen—the "Coasties"—would fish out the dead. And it was here, not in the war, that Webber hauled his first dead man over the thwart of a boat. The Chatham Bar took few prisoners.

It took none from the fishing vessel *Cachalot*. Two Chatham fishermen, Archie Nickerson and Elroy Larkin, had taken the *Cachalot* out the day before Halloween in 1950. Crossing the bar was always the most dangerous part of the trip. Outward bound, the trip was fine.

Coming in, all *seemed* fine. But as they approached the bar, one of those big ocean rollers came up from behind the *Cachalot* and upended her, end over end. The *Cachalot* tumbled forward and then came down with a thump upside down on the beach.

Bernie was among the first on the scene and recognized the body of Elroy Larkin. Nickerson was never found. It stunned Bernie. He knew the Chatham Bar could kill. But he had not seen firsthand the awesome strength of the ocean, the power of the waves on the bar to pitch-pole a 40-foot boat as if it were a tiddlywink flipped and spun by a thumb.

And this was not work done in anonymous commodities. This was personal. These dead men were friends. That's the way the Coasties felt about the town and the fishermen.

The town felt the same about the Coast Guard. It was not uncommon for the men to marry local Cape Cod girls. It was not uncommon for Chatham lads to seek careers in the Coast Guard. Many times the sons of drowned fishermen would do just that—make rescue work their life work, in homage to their lost dads. Larkin's son, Murray, did just that, enlisting in the Coast Guard and working on a cutter out of Woods Hole. Larkin's daughter, Esther, married a Coastie. Beverly Nickerson's daughter, Betty, was also to marry a Coast Guardsman who worked with Bernie.

So that is how it was. All of them in the fishing village knew the Coast Guard was there for them, that the Coasties would go out to their men in trouble when the water got rough. They knew that from what Frank

Masachi did two years earlier. Even if the Coast Guard brass did not know it sometimes, the town knew Masachi had done the right thing.

The Chatham Lifeboat Station had received the call on April 7, 1950, late at night as a seventy–mile per hour wind blew snow, sleet, and thunderous whitecaps into Cape Cod. Out there in the Atlantic, the fishing dragger *William J. Landry* was in big trouble with a boatload of fishermen onboard. The boat's wooden seams had opened to the sea in parts of her hull, and now the crew and captain were bailing madly to keep her afloat.

The Coast Guard took two actions. The officer in charge directed the *Landry* to head for the *Pollock Rip* lightship—a floating lighthouse run by the Coast Guard. There, Guy V. Emro, the ship skipper, would try to pass the boat a hawser, make it fast to the lightship, and get some pumps aboard. The officer also dispatched a small motorized lifeboat, just in case the lightship gambit did not work. Masachi would skipper it. Webber and two others would serve as crew.

Of the two boats available for the rescue, one was much closer. But the obvious and only choice was CG 36383, in Stage Harbor. The close boat—CG 36500—was in Old Harbor, a much shorter run to the *Landry* as the crow flies. But they could not follow the crow to the *Landry* because nothing in the water could cross the thunderous waves crashing down on the Chatham Bar. The storm had sealed Old Harbor. Nothing could challenge the bar and live.

So Masachi, Webber, Melvin G. Gouthro, and Antonio Ballerini set out for the Stage Harbor boat. The lifeboats were 36-foot affairs with a ton of bronze in the keel to keep them stable. A ninety-horsepower gas engine powered them surely, if slowly, through almost any sea. But because every inch of Chatham wharves were devoted to fishing vessels, the rescue boats were moored in the harbors and not kept dockside. So to reach them, the men first had to row out in a 19-foot dory.

Webber looked out at the harbor. Normally, it was quiet and protected. Tonight, it was a foamy torrent of whitecaps and storm-driven currents. They would be rowing directly into the wind and the waves and it would not be easy. Bernie Webber and Gouthro grabbed the oars and strained toward the CG 36383. They seemed frozen in time and space, hardly moving at all. One stroke forward seemed to carry them two back, so fierce was the wind. Webber's arms were throbbing and seemed pulled from his sockets when they reached the CG 36383. Eagerly the men reached out for the lifeboat—just as the waves hit the little dory dead wrong.

The boat flipped and the rescuers found themselves in peril. Suddenly, they were in freezing water, gasping in the cold. They reached out, all four of them, and grasped the overturned dory. No one was there to rescue them now and the danger of hypothermia was upon them. Men sometimes died in just fifteen minutes immersed in such water.

But they held on. They toed off their boots, which were heavy with water, and clung to the dory as they drifted in the blizzard. Soon, they saw they were drifting not toward the mainland but toward Morris Island, a deserted piece of land with only an old boathouse.

Numbed, with teeth chattering, they washed up on Morris Island. The men looked to the boathouse and were moving toward the shelter when Frank Masachi stopped them. Find the oars, he said. Right the boat. Let's carry it down the shore and try this again.

The men mumbled in disbelief, but they ought to have expected it. Masachi was old school. He had worked with some of the old surf men, and every one of them knew those stories. And they knew the motto.

Perhaps Patrick Etheridge represented the tradition the best. The legendary lifesaver—an African-American of Pea Island, North Carolina, on the Outer Banks—asked one of his men what the situation was one stormy day in 1898 regarding progress toward the rescue of passengers on a wrecked ship. The man looked out at the wreck, looked at the storm, looked at the huge waves and the rip and allowed as how, well, they could get out to the wreck fine, but they would never ever make it back.

Etheridge looked as if he was dealing with a dolt.

"The Blue Book says we've got to go *out*," he snapped at the man. "It doesn't say a damn thing about having to come *back*."

And in truth that is what the "book"—the manual for rescues—said. "The statement of the keeper that he did not try to use the boat because the sea or surf was too heavy will not be accepted unless attempts to launch it were actually made and failed ... If the device first selected fails ... he will resort to one of the others, and if that fails, then to the remaining one, and he will not desist from his efforts until by actual trial the impossibility of effecting a rescue is demonstrated."

And in one of his most famous of rescues, Etheridge did exactly that. At first, Etheridge tried to shoot a line to a wreck. Then he and his men tried rowing. The winds were too strong, the seas too rough. So finally, Etheridge tied lines to his men. They swam out, grabbed the passengers, and swam back through towering seas to safety.

In 1952, the Blue Book passages were exactly the same. Etheridge's words on the beach had morphed through the decades so that a half-century later the informal Coast Guard slogan was shorter and simpler. It went: You have to go out. You don't have to come back. And so, in that cold gale of April 7, 1950, Frank Masachi was seen neither as a zealot nor seriously imbalanced. He was just Coast Guard.

With no boots, barefooted, in soaking clothes, in a freezing blizzard, the men carried the dory 200 yards up the shore and set out again for the CG 36383.

Again, they strained against the oars. This time, they strained so hard that the thole pins, the holders of the oars, snapped. The dory veered in the high waves and strong currents and again overturned.

The men were again submersed into frigid water and exposed again to hypothermia. They held on again to the dory and washed up again on Morris Island. This time, to the relief of the crew, Frank walked directly to the boathouse and kicked in the door. Thank God they were done, Webber thought.

But then Masachi fired up the gas generator in the boathouse and his bedraggled crew stared back at him in various states of exposure and hypothermia. How was he going to get them out of this, off the island and in front of a warm fire? Was he calling for the DUKW, the amphibious vehicle that motored on land and water?

"Here," Masachi said, or in words very close to these. He had tossed them an old broom. "Use your knives. Whittle new thole pins. We're going back out to the boat."

Then he cranked up the magneto telephone and told the rescue operations leaders they were going to try again.

Soon they were back at the dory, launching again. This time, the thole pins held. But the oars did not. The very oars themselves cracked and splintered. The boat wheeled wildly and sent the men into the drink again, into the freezing cold water. They took the same frigid commute to the shore and washed up near the boathouse. Again, they banged through the door. Masachi, shivering, cranked the magneto again and called in. He confirmed the fishing vessel was still in peril, and then told his men they needed to keep trying.

Now, they were headed to the other lifeboat, the CG 36500, which could only go out over the Chatham Bar.

It was a suicide run. They all knew it. Masachi walked his men a mile, barefoot through the snow, to a narrow channel the men could wade. They left Morris Island and on the mainland were picked up by jeep. They made it back to the station, changed to dry clothes, and began to recover from exposure that would have hospitalized a sane man.

Then Masachi gave the orders. They were taking the other boat. They were heading to the CG 36500 and were going to run the Chatham Bar.

He means to kill us, Webber remembered thinking. *He is taking it personally and he will aid the* Landry *even it means our lives in the try.*

Bernie Webber wished with all his might that this would just go away, that he could run away from it. All of his Coast Guard training had not prepared him for this.

Then they all heard it on the radio and there was no time for thought. The *Landry* had rammed into the lighthouse boat and was damaged. The men on the fishing boat were exhausted. They had spent twenty-four hours fighting to stay alive and could no longer try to moor alongside the lightship. They would just wait for the lifeboat, for Masachi.

The transmission propelled Masachi and crew toward the door, and Webber moved to the door too. They had no choice. They had to go out. There were fishermen out there waiting for them and they lived in a town of fishermen.

But then they heard Captain Emro on board the lightship.

"Oh, my God …" he said quietly over the radio.

A huge wave had seized the little fishing vessel and spun it around. The *Landry*'s captain came on the radio in a very tired voice. More water was coming on. The men were oh-so-tired. The engine room was flooding.

"Boys," he said at last, "we're going down below to pray and have something to eat. If we die out here, it will be with full stomachs, so long, thank you. God bless you all."

"God be with you," Emro said.

Just a few minutes later, another wave washed over the *Landry* and she and her crew sank quickly beneath the black, storm-tossed sea.

There was a stunned silence in the Coast Guard rescue room in Chatham. All four of the rescuers were crushed. Webber could feel a deep ache in his heart. They had failed. He would have gone, he told himself. Wasn't he going when the boat sank?

But however you looked at it, they had failed.

They had failed and the next day, a contingent of Coast Guard brass from Boston was there to investigate why. The men were questioned sharply, one-by-one. Then all the rescuers were assembled and the officers from Boston aggressively interrogated them as a group. The chiefs and the enlisted men took it silently without defending themselves. They simply said they were unable to get to the lifeboat, without much explanation. They did not go into the repeated attempts. To a Coastie, it sounded like excuses. You have to go out. You *have* to go out.

It was Emro, the captain of the lightship, who finally intervened. A lieutenant was interrogating Masachi, and Emro could take it no more.

"*Goddamn it*! Who do you think you are?" he demanded of the officers from Boston.

Emro was thirty years at sea. He wore an old fashioned Coast Guard uniform with brass buttons turned green by salt spray. He strode into the center of the hearing hall and faced the three officers directly with eyes flashing under shaggy black and gray eyebrows.

How long had they been at sea?

What were they doing that night?

Were they safe in Boston? Were they snug in bed?

Well, Emro wasn't. He was on a very large lightship just inches from the fishing vessel, and the seas were so strong he was lucky to stay afloat himself.

And these men were not snug in bed either. They were floating in freezing water. Did the officers know, did the officers care, that the Coast Guard ship *Hornbeam* also could not make it to the *Landry*? A 180-foot ship couldn't make it and you're torturing these guys about swamping a 19-foot dory? They did their best.

They set out three times and would have gone four.

They were going to shoot the Chatham Bar!

"God*damn* it," Emro said in closing. "Who do you think you are?"

And that was it. It corked the investigation. The officers left shortly after that confrontation. No critical word ever was heard.

Except, of course, the words that the men heard in their own heads. Forget the fact that it was an impossible mission. They had failed. Fishermen had died. Each time they passed the *Pollock Rip* lightship, they felt a pang, a twinge of guilt.

And it was true, too, that each time the weather blew hard like it had that night in 1950, that the heartache would return to Webber.

Whenever, he saw the clouds move in hard and dark from the northeast like that—as they were now, in fact—Webber thought about the *Landry* and what they might have done differently. And how he admired Masachi and wished he could emulate him whenever he could. He saw Masachi and decided it one day. Webber did not want to have those thoughts about running, about hoping to avoid the dangerous rescues. He wanted to be as good as Masachi. He wanted to be that brave. He wanted to be just like him.

Well, there was a storm moving in now, on this February day of 1952. Soon they would be doing some non-routine work, that was for sure. Masachi had moved on to another assignment aboard a cutter, so they would have to carry on without him. The new guys who came in— Daniel W. Cluff and Donald Bangs—were a little looser than Masachi, a little more laid-back, a little less disciplined. But Webber already had his model in Frank Masachi. He thought about the man a lot, particularly on days like this.

Three

COLD STEEL

February 12–18, 1952
Aboard the *Pendleton* and *Fort Mercer*

All during the trip north, the *Pendleton* and the *Fort Mercer* steamed steadily in pace with one another, their officers not aware or caring particularly that the other ship was out there. They had no real meaning to each other. Just two ships out of hundreds.

Still, they were inextricably bound. For whether the crews knew it or not, whether the Coast Guard knew it or not, whether anyone cared or not, the two vessels were steaming toward a sort of "double blind" experiment of whether the American Bureau of Shipping was correct in stating that the crack arrestors would work.

The ships were nearly identical with the same cargoes heading for the same general destination at the same speed. Across the Gulf of Mexico, they sailed in warm temperatures in the seventies, then rounded Florida and made the turn toward New England and colder weather. They were two huge floating containers accompanied by dozens of others in the coastal trade. They moved oil and kerosene that helped power the frigid Northeast during the winter months.

Paetzel, onboard the *Fort Mercer*, knew T-2s had troubles but had faith in the crack arresters. He could see two of them on deck and knew two more were below on the hull. The big steel belts were recommended in 1947 to attempt to stop cracks from spreading in the T-2s. The ships were among the first all-welded vessels produced en masse in the war and mariners were suspicious of the welding process. Riveted ships with hulls of steel plating, each held together with steel pins, would suffer cracks but rarely casualties. The one plate might crack, but the crack would only run just through the plate, not the entire ship. The rivets would stop the crack, or the next plate over would hold firm.

Not so for the all-welded T-2s with nary a rivet in place. Welds did not stop cracks as rivets and plate-ends did. Welds might even create cracks, some thought. And once started, the cracks did not stop. They shot around the ship at the speed of sound.

The most dramatic example of what could go wrong was the *Schenectady*, a brand-new tanker that had been to sea trials in 1943 and was moored dockside. Without warning, in calm waters, she simply cracked in two. One crack raced through the girth of the ship in seconds and met itself in the middle. The *Schenectady* jackknifed down with her bow and stern pointing toward the sky, still moored dockside.

Everyone thought bad welding was the problem. Everyone was pretty much wrong. Welding was visible and villainized but at best played a bit role. The problem, discovered only years later, lay not in something so obvious or visible, but at the molecular level. In 1954, tests would show conclusively that the steel used in the wartime ships contained too much sulfur and behaved badly in cold water. The steel worked fine in riveted ships, but not in all-welded ships. Not at certain times, at least.

When it became too cold, the metal hulls began behaving differently. It was far less ductile. Normally, steel flexes. The whole ship bends and moves with the sea. But the ductility in this steel ("mild steel" it was called by some, "dirty steel" by others) changed with temperature. The colder it got, the more the steel took on the characteristics of crystal rather than a ductile, flexible metal. It became brittle. Taffy may stretch at room temperature; freeze it and it will shatter when hit with a hammer. In a sense, that is what was happening to the steel in the *Pendleton*'s hull.

At the time the *Pendleton* and the *Fort Mercer* sailed, officials mostly just knew when the ships were most likely to fracture, not why. Mostly those times were (a) when it got cold, and (b) when it got rough.

And now, the *Pendleton* and the *Fort Mercer*, far from the eighty-degree weather of Louisiana, were going where it was both rough and cold. They were heading into colder water and the nature of the steel of the hull was transformed from something that could give and take under the stress of waves to something that caved in and cracked.

The two tankers first felt the brunt of the gale as they rounded Long Island on February 16. The storm was bad, but both ships had weathered far worse. Captain Fitzgerald onboard the *Pendleton* saw no need to alter course, nor did Captain Paetzel onboard the *Fort Mercer*. Miles apart, casually aware of each other on their radars, they both kept forward speed with the props rotating between forty-five and sixty-five revolutions per minute, depending on conditions.

They passed Nantucket and Martha's Vineyard and moved north on February 17 as the storm worsened. The two ships came even with Chatham and Bernie Webber's little outpost, noting the lightships that guarded Chatham Bar and Pollock Rip and marked the dangerous currents at the elbow of Cape Cod. There was a new experimental radar machine at the Coast Guard station and it may have picked up the T-2s as they passed and headed for their ports of call. The new system was glitchy. A technician was there to tweak it, in fact. It worked, then didn't; worked, then didn't.

At Race Point, near the tip of the Cape, the paths of the two ships diverged finally, each heading to her port of call. But once there—the *Pendleton* outside Boston, the *Fort Mercer* outside Portland, Maine— visibility was next to nothing and the storm had worsened.

Independent of one another, each captain came to the same careful decision: docking in this sort of weather was not worth the risk. It would be much easier to ride out the storm overnight in deep water and come into port on a sunnier day. Ships bumped into things in ports when visibility was so poor. Or they bumped bottom in shallow water if they missed channel markers.

In the deep waters off the Cape lay safety. The ships would pitch and buck in the waves there but they would come to no harm as there was nothing hard to hit. The *Fort Mercer* turned south from Maine and took up a position about twenty-five miles off Cape Cod. The *Pendleton* took a similar bearing from Boston and turned her bow into the waves keeping just enough forward movement to maintain steering and stability. She was a bit farther north of the *Fort Mercer* and a bit closer to the Cape but under full control. Both ships turned slightly into the waves at an angle and kept up power so the bow split the waves. It was a big blow but each ship had handled much bigger ones.

This was all routine, and the crews of both ships settled into the routine. The deck officers and able seamen stood watch on the forward bridge, four hours on, four hours off, as was the tradition. Farther back in the stern section, the engineers and oilers and wipers toiled deep below decks keeping the boiler fires burning, the steam coming, and the smooth electrical drives turning the powerful props. Someone measured the ocean temperature. It varied between thirty-eight and forty-two degrees that night. The winds were fifty miles per hour and the waves, some of them, crested at 30 to 45 feet.

Still, this was no big deal. Yes, in years past, thousands of sail vessels had crashed on that leeward shore in storms just like this. A dismasting, a loss of a rudder, a sudden failure of wooden seams and a ship was quickly blown into the surf line. Running ashore was not salvation; it was ruin. Ships would drag bottom hundreds of yards from safety and the waves would pound the ship and the men into the sand.

But that was then and this was now—in the age of steam and power. The *Fort Mercer* and the *Pendleton* took the seas just fine. The strong and sturdy bows would plunge and be buried by the sea, then explode back into the air, buoyant, triumphant, pointing toward Boston, toward Maine—just waiting for the storm to clear a bit. Most of the crew expected to be on land in two hours. That's where their thoughts were: already on shore.

Chief Engineer Sybert in the engine compartment of the *Pendleton* kept the prop spinning just as Captain Fitzgerald had signaled him with a series of bells that were activated by wires that ran from the forward bridge to the engine room astern. Sometimes Fitzgerald would ring to speed up, sometimes to slow down. The bells told the engine room what the bridge desired.

She was handling nicely, Sybert thought, but early in the morning, before 5 a.m., a heavy sea washed over the poopdeck. It was nothing really, but notable enough to call to the bridge. If they changed watch and sent seamen back from the forward bridge to the stern quarters, they could be in real trouble. Sybert told Fitzgerald something like, "We've got seas over the poopdeck; best not to send anyone back aft on the catwalk else they might get drenched."

Fitzgerald acknowledged the seas; he had already seen them. He told Sybert that he had sent the seamen down to get coffee in the forward salon. But thanks for the heads up.

Thus did little decisions above the decks of the *Pendleton* affect the fate of the crew as, below the decks, in the hull itself, very small changes in the steel would have a profound impact upon them all.

The men may have been warm aboard the *Pendleton* but the *Pendleton*'s steel was far too cold. And with 35-foot waves, that steel was most certainly being hammered and stressed.

It was cold. It was rough. The two factors that accompanied most T-2 crack-ups weren't just present, they were prevalent.

At around 5:50 a.m., Sybert felt the ship take a heavy lurch. There was an explosive bang, very loud. Then Sybert felt an even heavier lurch and the explosive sound this time was even louder than the first bang.

Others felt it more than heard it: a sound, a force, a pulse of energy. Another said it was a tearing sound. They were not sure what it was, only that "it" was not good.

Did it take five minutes? one of the men was asked later.

"Five seconds," he replied.

Sybert felt the ship roll heavily and take a list to port. Then she straightened. It was normal again.

Thank God everything seemed okay. The one problem was he could not reach the captain to find out what Fitzgerald wanted done, to see what had happened. The signals were dead and so were the phones. Had they run aground? Struck something? Sybert needed instructions now. How fast? How slow? Forward? Reverse? What did Captain Fitzgerald want? There were no bells.

So Sybert dispatched oilier Tchuda W. Southerland to the deck to see if he could make his way forward to contact Fitzgerald. Ask the captain what we should do, Sybert said, but be careful on the catwalk moving forward. The waves had been breaking over the ship at times.

And when Southerland got topside he was careful. He ran slowly forward toward the bridge against the ripping gale—and found there was not a forward there. He gaped out at the emptiness where the forward part of the ship had been and then was distracted. Another ship was close by them. Too close. He stood on the stern section of the *Pendleton* and looked at the bow of the second ship. Painted there clear as day was the word "Pendleton."

But *he* was on the *Pendleton* and there was a split-second before he understood that he was looking at the free-floating bow of his ship, and that the *Pendleton* had split in two at the number 7 and 8 tanks.

About the same time, Pumpman James E. Young was awakened from sleep and thought the ship had just taken a heavy lurch. He went to the mess where everyone else was. The ship's split, they said. He did not believe it and rushed topside. Instantly, he was scared. The gale knocked him about and the wind and ice and snow stung him. And there was the

29

bow. Unmistakably. He rushed back down to confirm the bad news to Sybert.

Sybert already knew it. He had glanced out from his cabin through the porthole there and seen an odd sight. It was the bow of the *Pendleton*. He could see Fitzgerald there. It was unmistakably the captain. He was fighting to keep his balance, grabbing for the rail as the bow pitched and bucked in the waves.

Sybert took stock. The officers were stranded on the front part of the ship, the bow section. The engineers and most of the crew were in the stern section.

Circuit breakers had kicked out all electricity to the forward part of the vessel, while the machinery in the rear continued as if normal. The stern section resembled a hotel that had had one wall blown away. The cross section of the ship was exposed to the elements but still functioning and to an extent seaworthy, even in a gale.

Sybert kept up steam, ordered watertight hatches closed, and closed down the electrical power for a moment as a precaution. Then he summoned everyone to the mess room.

The bow of the *Pendleton*, bridge awash in waves.

All of them waited for an explosion. Their kerosene and heating oil had sprung from the tanks when the ship halves separated. Hell, they were tanker men. Death by explosion was foreordained.

But the fire never came. The wind was too strong. It whipped away the fumes. Or the break—so complete and large—dispelled the fumes quickly so no magical and deadly mixture of oxygen, gas vapors, and spark created the traditional tanker bomb. For these things the men on the stern could be thankful.

The officers on the bow, on the other hand, were in a different world—without time for an SOS, without time for anything. The men were stranded on the bridge of the ship with no way to life rafts or lifeboats. The bow pitched and bucked at a forty-five-degree angle to the sea. It was buffeted, swept and raked by heavy seas. What had been the command center of the ship was now more like a beach at storm tide. Breakers swept over it. The bow-half bobbed about, tilting evermore toward a vertical plane. On the stern, Sybert brought power back up. He discovered he could actually steer the ship—a bit. He had power. He had a rudder. She would buck and heave, but for brief moments he could control the ship.

The thought had to strike Sybert there and then. It was strange, but there it was. He was master of a ship, his half-ship. He had given a command, maneuvered her, and she responded. He was a master.

He took command. But there was one problem with that—and he quickly confessed it. He gathered all the survivors in the mess and told it to them straight: Boys, our officers are gone and you able-bodied seamen are going to have to pick up the slack. I know engines. Don't know much about navigation, lifeboats, and seamanship in general.

Quickly, he found that one able-bodied seaman, Jacob Hicks, and another, Ray Steele, would take leadership positions. He came to think of Hicks as a makeshift chief mate, the ranking deck officer.

Did Sybert want them to check the lifeboats? Yes, Sybert said, but he thought the best thing to do was remain on board the stern section of the ship if it seemed seaworthy. Others were dispatched to close all water-tight doors. Sybert and his engineers checked the salinity of the boilers to see if too much seawater had leaked in.

Hicks and Steele scrambled up on the deck and what they saw and felt there was disheartening. The gale was now a full-blown screeching storm with winds of fifty miles per hour and more. It would reach more than seventy before the night was through, reports said, sometimes clocked at eighty. You had to lean into a wind like that just to stand steady.

They struggled to reach the lifeboats and once there, prepared them for launch. But below them—sometimes over them—soared waves of 35 to 45 feet. Launching a lifeboat into such mountains of water would be fearsome work. It would be a miracle just to get a boat out there without the sea splintering it. Once launched, how long could a small lifeboat remain afloat?

They seemed stuck staying with the stern.

They looked across the water toward the bow. The bow and all the deck officers on it were carried swiftly away from the stern by the moun-tainous waves. The bow section was still afloat but increasingly it rose at an angle to the plane of the sea, lifting the bow to the sky, plunging the bridge and deckhouse down toward the bottom. In fifteen to twenty minutes, the bow disappeared from view, bobbing away into the rain and snow, invisible to the men on the stern now.

Sybert was certain they would get help soon. The radioman had almost certainly sent an SOS from the bridge.

It took time for it to sink in that this was improbable and that no one on shore was aware any of this was happening. Slowly, they were under-standing the fix they were in.

The splitting of the ship was clear enough; the ramifications of the split less so. Yes, the captain and most deck officers were located toward the front of the ship in a structure that rose from the deck and gave them a clear view ahead. The engineers and engine room were located aft. So the officers were gone but the clean fracture had wrought even worse chaos. The bow had the radio but no power; Sybert's new half-ship had the power but no radio.

Sybert did the math. The ship had split apart in about five seconds. There could not have been time, no time at all, to understand what was happening and send out a signal. Sybert thought they were close to shore. They had been nearly twenty-five miles offshore due east of northern Cape Cod, but their drift was south and west now, which would take them quickly toward the elbow of Cape Cod, toward Chatham. That fact had been a blessing initially and somehow comforting. But now?

He could maneuver the stern section a bit, but he knew they were drifting *too* rapidly toward shore—the Cape Cod shore where so many thousands of wrecks had washed up. If he attempted to steer and control too aggressively, the ship would pitch and lurch. There was little he could do other than go with the flow and steer to keep the stern section straight. He could not steam her farther out to sea, just keep her straight as she drifted. Every time he attempted to steer and maneuver, he could, briefly, but the forward exposed part of the stern dipped down and got drenched.

Above him, on deck, Hicks dug out a flare gun from the lifeboat. He pointed it skyward and the flare arched out over the water into the darkness. Perhaps they would be spotted visually from shore. Perhaps the officers on the bow would respond with a flare back. He took out another flare cartridge and aimed it skyward. The cartridge fizzled and popped but did not fire. From the bow, no reply came at all. Hicks looked at the date stamped on the flares: July 1942. He threw the dud flare into the water after it had fizzled. He loaded another. No luck. No signals. He took smoke markers from the lifeboat and lit them, then tossed them overboard. They put out a pathetic smudge of smoke that was quickly whipped away to nothing in the gale.

No radio. No flares. No smoke. No blinker lights for sending code. No one who could send or understand code, either.

No one knew they were out there. No one knew they were in trouble. No one had any way of finding out.

Well, there was one way, one ancient way.

Aaron Powell, a wiper, rigged up a line to the steam whistle. Another wiper was too small a man to work the rig himself; it took some heft to pull the line. So Powell drafted George "Tiny" Myers, an OS, ordinary seaman. He weighed more than three hundred pounds, not much of it muscle, it had to be said, but Tiny had plenty of spirit and enough weight to heave that whistle lanyard.

They were not sure what the true navigational whistle signals were for their situation but kept blowing and blowing and blowing. The danger signal was all Powell knew… a series of short blasts. They would blast out four short signals and then pause to listen for any reply.

There was none. They were alone.

Four

DISCOVERY

February 18, 1952
Chatham Lifeboat Station—5:00 a.m. to 3:00 p.m.

Webber was warm inside the Chatham Lifeboat Station and coffee was percolating on the mess-deck stove. Outside, the gale was gaining strength, it seemed, and howling for their attention. He had mixed feelings as he always did on such nights. They were rescuers, and that is what they did. So storms meant business. Action.

Firemen had to have the same feelings. You did not want conflagrations. On the other hand, it was part of what you lived for, and if you had none, ever, what was the point?

Certainly there was a small voice in Webber saying, *Please, God, not another* Landry. *Don't make me go into the cold, cold water like that again.*

Then there was another voice that sounded a lot like Masachi's and it *wanted* another *Landry*—wanted to make the *Landry* rescue good, to do it over again, to have a happy ending. Fill in the holes in their hearts that the *Landry* sank into.

It would seem a natural thing, remorse over lost seamen. But in the Coast Guard, remorse became magnified to something more. In a culture where one had to go out but one need not come back, there was a stigma to those who came back without rescuing those in peril. And this stigma seemed to attach itself even in the most unfair cases.

Nothing illustrated that better than the case of David Atkins, the heroic keeper of a Cape lifesaving station near Provincetown. In April 1879, a coal-carrying schooner, the *Sarah J. Fort*, foundered a quarter mile off shore. Atkins led his team to rescue the ship's crew and officers by shooting a line from a small cannon out to the ship. The lifesaver was skilled in the use of the gear of its time, the Parrot Gun. A new, more efficient cannon had recently arrived—the Lyle Gun—but Atkins was not familiar with its operation.

In the gale that blew, the Parrot Gun could not reach the ship. Eventually, lifesavers reached the ship by boat and saved many of those on board, but lost many as well.

An inquiry specifically stated that Atkins had done all he could, but also noted that had he been able to use the more modern Lyle Gun, he might have saved more people. It had more range. It might have gotten a line out there. The inquiry board held him blameless and praised his courage, but Atkins himself felt huge self-guilt. Nor was it helped by the townspeople of Provincetown who, he said, subjected him and his crew to the "goading slur." What was in their behavior or his mind is unclear, but there was no doubt that the goading slur was real to him.

Next season, he said to his wife, he would redeem himself and end the goading slur—or die in the trying.

He did both. In November 1880, he led a crew to rescue those stranded on the *C.E. Tribal*. He hauled a boatload back to shore, but on the return trip for more, the lifesaving boat capsized and Atkins was lost.

So a man of great courage and heroism had been held in disgrace, in his own eyes at least. History redeemed his reputation, but made it only clearer that on the ground, in real time, this was a culture of extremes. You had to go out, you did not have to come back. If you came back empty-handed, you might just as well have stayed out.

So yes, this was a culture of courage. It could also be a culture of cruelty.

Some of Webber's tension this day was relieved when he got an important assignment inside the harbor. Warrant Officer Cluff, the new guy, gave it to him. The Virginian said in his thick drawl that Webber and a crew needed to get the CG 36500 going and check the harbor for boats torn loose from their moorings.

This was almost as important work as saving lives. It saved livelihoods. Webber knew the fishermen of the town would be crowded down at the Fish Pier, squinting through the windows, huddled around the woodburning stove, trying to see whether their boats were still safe and sound.

The stakes were high. Some of the fishermen were so down on their luck they'd borrow gasoline from the Coast Guard, and then pay it back if a catch came in. This storm was screeching through the harbor now and if their fishing vessels were drifting ashore, the boats would be broken to bits by the waves, and the fishermen and their families would be penniless.

Given the givens, this was familiar stuff and the only assignment, really, for the CG 36500. She was the boat that faced the Chatham Bar. No way anyone was crossing the bar in this sort of storm. If anything, this one was far worse than the *Landry* storm. One difference was the storm hit differently than the *Landry* storm, so the harbor had better shelter. The men rowed the dory to the bigger boat without incident. The CG 36500 handled the harbor waters just fine and they were not going anywhere near the open sea. It was all harbor work.

Still, it was cold work and hard work. They were at it for several hours. Several of the boats had broken loose. They taxied the CG 36500 from one to the other. The lifeboat had a ton of bronze in its keel and it did not move quickly. But once it was underway, its Sterling Petrel ninety-horsepower motor provided deep torque and purchase in the water. The covered part of the lifeboat could hold up to twenty survivors sheltered from the elements. She could also tow a lot, the CG 36500, and with that bronze in her keel, she was self-righting. Officially, the Coast Guard rated the boat class "unsinkable." A wave could roll her over, and if you hung on tight, she would turn right side up, eventually. If you hung in there and held your breath while you were wrong side down.

In these harbor waters, rollovers were not a worry. You had to be careful, but it was no big deal. Truth of it was, Bernie was pretty good at this stuff and the CG 36500 had become his favorite boat. She was the first 36-footer he had seen in his career and he felt a certain special feeling about her.

Was Bernie as good as Bangs? Probably not. Not yet. But there was no doubt Bernie Webber was good. With any luck now, he might be able to cut out for home and check on Miriam, his wife. She had been sick with the flu for two days, but he had been on duty. It would be nice to be able to check in on her, to take care of her.

He was getting the hang of this married stuff now. It had settled him. He was no longer the lost young lad easily led. The Coast Guard and marriage had built his character.

But, brother, had that taken some time. If he had been confused during his teenage years, his dating days were pure chaos and it was only through the grace of God that he had met Miriam, now sniffling and coughing back in their cozy apartment in Chatham.

Two years earlier, he and some friends from the station had set out for Provincetown, at the tip of Cape Cod, to meet some P-town girls. The Provincetown scene was much wilder than Chatham, and Webber's intentions may not have been wholly honorable.

But the car full of would-be rakes got no farther than Orleans, a good forty-five minutes from Provincetown, when the car threw a rod. Webber, the preacher's son, dialed the operator and tracked down the young women in Provincetown. He was ever so polite and such a gentleman as he explained the situation and apologized that they could not make the dates.

Such a display of manners may have been lost on the P-towners, but they were not lost entirely. For a few days later, a woman called the Coast Guard station asking for someone she thought was named Webster. They figured that had to be Bernie and so they transferred the call to him. The young woman was both shy and direct. She had heard a lot about him, that he was nice. Had a nice voice, had nice manners.

Hey, Bernie replied, if you've heard so much about me, why don't you know my name? The young man was flabbergasted. Only two days before, he was pursuing a young woman in Provincetown, and now, it seemed, this young woman was pursuing him.

What's your name? he asked. "Wait a sec," she said, and there was a pop and crackle on the line. Then she was back to him and said essentially: "I have to get to know you better before I tell you my name. Can I call you back?"

Webber was reluctant. But there were long, long one-man watches where he just killed time on the ten-to-two shift late at night. She could call then.

She did. Night after night. They talked about everything and she learned Webber's life story. She knew everything. He did not even know her name. Always, she would call and they would talk for hours. But every few minutes she would say, "Wait a sec" and there would be that pop and click, a pause, and she would be back a moment later.

Finally, Webber had enough. He still did not know her name. "Listen," he said, "we have to meet or you have to stop calling me. I have to know how you found out about me and I have to meet you."

"Wait a sec," she said. And then she agreed to a meeting, with her parents' consent, at a drug store in Wellfleet, halfway down the Cape toward P-town, "How did you know about me?" he asked. "You have to tell me that, too."

She paused. "Wait a sec." She was back and said essentially, "I was the telephone operator the night your car broke down. I listened in on your call and you sounded like a really nice guy, but I had to check you

39

out. I call you when I'm at work and business is slow. I talk to you in between calls."

And so they met. Webber and a friend went to the pharmacy-soda fountain on the weekend. He saw a girl at the counter, but when she spoke, Bernie knew it wasn't Miriam. She's back there, the woman said, pointing toward a phone booth. All Webber could see was fur and hair. It filled the phone booth. The sight scared him. He had a blind date with Bigfoot!

And then Bigfoot turned around. She was wearing a fur coat with her back to him. She was dressed to the nines. Long blond hair, piercing blue eyes.

And Webber thought she was the most beautiful woman he had ever seen. A funny feeling came over him then. He got on the good side of her strict parents when he said he was the son of a minister, and the young man and woman were "sanctioned." They saw each other every time they could, and on one date, in the car, Miriam turned dreamily to Webber and proposed to him.

Webber clutched. He was not expecting this. This, he did not have the hang of, did not even know there was a hang to it. He stuttered, sweated, then blurted out, "No!"

Fine, Miriam said. She was crushed. "You should take me home then," she said.

Webber started the car and prepared to back out and head home. His head was clearing and he realized what she had said, what he had said. He did not want to lose her. He loved her. Besides, he thought, it was winter. They drove along silently.

"Okay," Bernie said.

"Okay what?" Miriam said.

The marriage thing, Bernie said. When do you want to get married? He was thinking this year, next year? In the spring, in the fall?

Without a beat, she shot back, "July 16."

Bernie nodded.

"Okay, July 16," he said. But he quickly added that he needed the permission of his commanding officer under Coast Guard regulations.

He got it, and they were wedded on July 16, 1950. It had gone considerably smoother since then. They had moved into a rented house in Chatham nicknamed Silver Heels and had become a part of the close-knit community of seafaring families. The boats towed by the CG 36500 that night were more than boats. They were the businesses of dear friends and neighbors.

Now, if he could just get the fishing vessels taken care of, there was just enough time to pop home and tuck Miriam in and perhaps give her something for the vicious case of flu that left her feverish and sick.

But it took longer than he thought to return the stray fishing vessels and make certain they were secure to moorings and piers. The storm was a blizzard now, spitting alternate pellets of frozen rain and slanting sleet. The men were soaked and tired when they finally tied up the 36500 and returned to the lifeboat station in the afternoon. Bernie was looking forward to something hot to eat and perhaps some rest. His crew had put in a tough day's work already.

Then and only then did they get word that there might be work for them off shore. There would not be time to check on his sick wife, to show Miriam how he felt. The word was there was a big ship in trouble.

The word, when it first came, came not from the *Pendleton*, but from her twin, the *Fort Mercer*. The *Pendleton*, drifting in two halves now for nearly four hours, still lay undiscovered because the men aboard could not radio for help.

The *Fort Mercer* was not in great distress as yet, and she still had her radio. The word was not definitive—but only that she was experiencing some trouble. The officers were not certain. She might, in fact, be splitting in two.

They were not sure. Could the Coast Guard send help just in case?

Five

TWO DOWN

February 18, 1952
Aboard the SS *Fort Mercer*—8:00 a.m.

T he *Pendleton*'s crack-up began and ended in seconds. On the *Fort Mercer*, it began with a puzzle that solved itself only hours later.

Shifts, or watches, changed every four hours on the *Fort Mercer*. So at 8 a.m., a new bunch of officers and seamen trudged to the bridge and those on the old watch stepped down. The off-duty seamen would return aft, navigating the catwalk back to the deckhouse near the rear of the ship; off-watch officers generally would return to their quarters in the forward deckhouse.

So Perley W. Newman, a quartermaster, had just joined the bridge when he heard a metallic snap, a cracklike noise.

"What was that?" Captain Paetzel said. At first he thought that Newman had slammed the door hard. He was more annoyed than alarmed.

"I think the ship cracked," Newman replied.

"My God, I hope not," Paetzel said.

Newman craned his neck around looking backward toward his ship for damage.

The crew and officers had little problem confirming something was wrong. Thomas Gill, the first assistant engineer, was eating breakfast when he heard a sharp snapping sound. He rushed up to the deck to look around. He looked out and sure enough, there was heating oil leaking from the tanker—but only a small amount. He hailed the chief engineer who noted it almost routinely. No big deal, Gill thought, and he went back to finish his breakfast.

Paetzel too could see the oil leaking and knew there was some problem with the ship. Some tank or something had given away. His first thought was to inform the Coast Guard but not panic his crew. He had been a wartime officer. He knew that panic could be the worst enemy here. What if they rushed for the lifeboats? What if they tried to launch them?

At such times as these, Paetzel knew the lifeboats were all but useless. The seas were steep and breaking, up to 45 feet high sometimes. Some wave measurement instruments later would show them peaking at 60 feet.

So if you were lowering a boat into such waves, here is what you faced. At one moment, the top of a wave the height of a four-story building would be just even with you. The next moment, the trough of the wave would be 30 to 40 feet below you.

Time it right and you might launch a boat in conditions like this one time out of a hundred. But then what for this small boat with no cover in waves far larger than the boat itself?

He'd lose at least half the crew, he figured. At least twenty men. Better for them to take their chances on the ship.

So he called the Coast Guard then and told them his position and that he needed assistance. No, he said, he could not say he was in dire straits. But he needed the Coast Guard to be ready in case he needed them.

Confirm that, the Coast Guard station at Chatham replied, and Cluff told Paetzel he was dispatching cutters to the area and asking all ships at sea to stand by and assist. Helicopters were not widely used yet by the

Coast Guard and fixed-wing seaplanes could never land in such waves. So this would be a ship-to-ship affair. The good news was that there were several cutters in the general area. They had been searching for a fishing vessel, the *Paolina*, and another, the *Julia K*.

The *Eastwind*, a 269-foot cutter that was actually a polar icebreaker, was nearby. She had one problem in these seas. She'd been called upon to break ice in the Hudson River—an unusual chore during an unusually harsh winter. And to do that, the *Eastwind* had dumped ballast water so she only drew about 22 feet of water. Heading back to Boston, she kept the shallower trim and did not reballast because she was going to take a full load of diesel and head north to the Arctic.

This meant that the icebreaker, a big "roller" to begin with in normal weather, was really lively in the seas of this storm. She had difficulty maintaining good headway and at times bobbed side to side, almost like a buoy.

The cutter *Unimak* was in Boston when she got the call to assist. It was a casual enough alert that Commander Frank McCabe invited his father and eleven-year-old son along for the ride.

The *Legare* and the *Frederick Lee* were smaller cutters and scoured the ocean for the two missing fishing vessels but soon found that 125-foot ships were no matches for 40-foot waves. Both were ordered back to base, such was the pounding they received.

Two other cutters—the *Acushnet* and the *McCulloch*—might also be brought into play. The *Acushnet*, at dockside in Portland, Maine, heard the first *Fort Mercer* distress call and began preparations for sailing south. Such were the conditions that the deckhands found they could not cast off the hawsers from the dock. They struggled with the huge frozen dock lines, then took fire axes to them and cut their ship lose from the icy mooring.

Cluff forwarded the distress call to First District Headquarters in Boston and the response was prompt and clear. The *Eastwind* and *Unimak* would cease the fishing vessel searches and head for the *Fort Mercer*.

Later, the *Acushnet* was ordered to delay its scheduled overhaul and head south as well. The *Yakutat*, holed up in Provincetown Harbor, was dispatched at 1 p.m.

So that was the good news. There seemed no bad news. Yes, the cutters were heading toward the *Fort Mercer* through 120 miles of high seas. But there was no absolute urgency to the *Fort Mercer*'s plight. Paetzel had told his crew to stand by, but he sounded no general alarms. Panic was the enemy here, so far as he was concerned.

Still, Cluff, Bangs, and Bernie Webber stayed close to the radio that morning. You could never tell what might come up. The thought of sending 36-foot boats into 45-foot waves was unlikely—at least not 25 miles out to sea. So it was good that the cutters were at hand. Even the cutters were taking a beating. The *Yakutat*, up front, lost two steel doors to the storm, just pounded in by the weight of seawater slamming into supposedly watertight doors.

Not everyone on board the *Fort Mercer* felt as comfortable with the crack arrestors as the captain. Not everyone, in fact, felt comfortable with the captain.

Paetzel had ordered the men to be alert but had not sounded a general alarm. He did not want to sound any signals or bells that would stampede the crew. Word got out to some, but not to others. What followed was a combination of undue concern by some and unwarranted complacency among others.

Julio Molino, a seaman, was one of those who heard nothing from the master about the 8 a.m. crack. He did not have to be told. He was standing with a friend and looked out at sea.

"Look in the water, the ship is broke," Molino said matter of factly. "There's oil."

"I don't want to look," his friend said. "I'm scared."

"Let's go tell the captain," Molino said. But his friend was too scared and would not even look at the oil. He turned away from the sight.

Then Molino saw what he thought was a steel plate from the hull float away.

These guys are all too scared of the old man, Molino thought, because the captain is too tough on them. Well, the hell with it; Molino would tell him. He marched forward to the bridge and confronted the master of the ship—a rare and unthinkable breach of etiquette on most ships.

"What do *you* want?" Paetzel asked him on the bridge.

"The ship is broke," Molino said.

"That's none of your fucking business," Molino heard Paetzel say. And then the captain physically pushed the seaman off the master's bridge and toward the stairs.

None of my fucking business? It was completely Molino's business.

He ran down, got his life preserver, and began yelling out to anyone he could see, "The ship is broke!"

Jack C. Brewer, the chief mate and second in command after the captain, chased him down and cornered Molino.

"Who are you to tell the crew?" the mate demanded.

"I've been at sea long enough to know when there's danger," Molino said.

The bo'sun, William Joseph Heroux, intervened at this point. The bo'sun is the equivalent of a sergeant at sea—the head non-commissioned officer, so to speak, in charge of the deck crew. He channeled Molino's fears in a constructive manner.

"Take the covers off the boats," he told Molino. And Molino did just that. He ran to the starboard lifeboat at the stern and cut the cover off the boat. Then he jumped in. The quartermaster moved to swing the boat out and lower it. The starboard side was taking the most wind.

"Calm down, calm down!" the bo'sun said. "Move to the port side."

And Molino did. There was far less wind on that side of the ship. He prepared the boat there for launching, but this time he did not jump in. He stood watch for two hours, never leaving the side of the boat, but grew too cold and eventually went below.

About the time Molino went below, around 10:15 a.m., the *Fort Mercer* steel snapped again, with a loud gunlike sound. Robert Mackenzie, a seaman, heard three reports, loud, as if a machine gun had squeezed off three rounds. On the bridge, Newman turned to the purser and said, "That sounds bad."

Paetzel again radioed in the news. The ship continued to handle well. But below them, they could see heating oil pulsing out like arterial blood from a ruptured artery.

They stayed the course. They stayed their watches, too. Every four hours, the seamen would rotate in and new officers would man the bridge. Paetzel stayed through all watches in this emergency situation. He'd been on his feet so long that he went down briefly to his quarters and took off his big boots and exchanged them for a comfortable pair of loafers. He was a big man, heavy, and this little gesture gave him a moment's relief from aching feet.

At 11:40 a.m., the *Fort Mercer* crew heard a third loud report and they saw a crack run up the starboard side of the number 5 tank several feet above the waterline. Paetzel sent out an urgent message now for all vessels nearby to stand by to come to the aid of the *Fort Mercer*.

Still, the noon shift occurred without fanfare. Newman left the bridge and said to his relief man, Louis Culver, "Don't let her go amidships, keep her into the sea."

Newman went aft to the galley and was sipping soup when he heard another snap, a terrific crack of noise and a palpable surge of energy. He knew instantly what this was and rushed topside.

Down below, Tony "Pumps" Roviaro, the chief pumpman, was working with the chief engineer. They heard the snap, the crack, and felt the pulse of energy and thump through the hull. There was a pause. Then Chief Engineer Jesse Bushnell said, "Pumps, I think one of the tanks amidships is crushed."

"Yes, I think so too," Roviaro said.

Did the captain give any alarm? Roviaro asked that question, but no one seemed to know. He put on a life jacket and yelled back to the chief, "I think she cracked up."

He ran onto the deck to hear one of the boys say, "Oh, there's another ship ahead of us."

"Heck no," someone else said. "That's the *Fort Mercer* floating …"

For certain, along the side of the "other ship" was the name "Fort Mercer." But how could that be? They were *on* the *Fort Mercer*.

Then, just as on the *Pendleton*, there was a rush to realization as to how worlds had changed. They had split in two, cleanly in two. And then there was a sense of pure panic. A wave came up on the bow of the *Fort Mercer* and cleanly sheared away the two lifeboats there. The men on the stern could see that. Then the bow began drifting directly back to the stern, on a collision path, it seemed.

Word went down to Bushnell in the engine room and the chief engineer gently backed the engines astern. The smooth electro glide nature of the T-2 was still there; the half-ship responded and Bushnell maneuvered out of harm's way. The act—one half of a ship avoiding collision with its other half—is believed unique in known maritime history.

On the stern, the men did not commemorate this historic event. They were excited, nearly a mob. They rushed the lifeboats. They were crowded around the starboard lifeboat, intent on piling in, lowering the boats and getting off the ship any way they could. The wind was blowing directly into them—the spray and snow and rain pelting them.

Laurence Whilley, an ordinary seaman, was there when a man from the mess (he did not know his name) yelled to Whilley above the howling weather: "Do you know how to pray?"

"Sure, I'm a Christian and a member of the church," Whilley yelled back. "No one should be ashamed to pray."

The man and Whilley left the boat and went to the mess. There they got down on their knees and prayed for their lives, prayed for the men, prayed for the ship, and prayed for their world.

Above, the bo'sun looked at the men jostling the lifeboats, looked at the surging seas, looked at the relative calm and steadiness of the stern and told the quartermaster, "Tell the boys to take it easy."

Roviaro, the pumpman, ran to the stern above the men and yelled out, "There's no danger." And Newman, the quartermaster, chimed in, "Take it easy; it's too rough a sea." Then seaman Robert Mackenzie yelled a flat-out order. "Don't touch the boat!"

"Don't get excited," the quartermaster yelled again. "Let's see what we can do."

All of those men kept cautioning the crew. Let's see what we can do with the stern, which seemed steady, all things considered. There's too much wind on the starboard side, someone added. Why are we here?

"Let's try the port side," someone else said.

"We'll do that," the bo'sun said.

And the men moved over to the port side, the more sheltered side, and again this seemed to calm them just as it had Molino earlier. Soon, thoughts of taking the boats had subsided. They made sure the port boat was prepared and then went down below. It was more stable and calming there. Darkness fell and the stern still seemed steady. The mess was open for business. It was warm. In many ways, it was normal. Comforting this, the warmth and the coziness of the mess.

Still, it was a long night, sleepless for most. In the morning, there was word from above that lights had been sighted. A plane flew over. A bit later and the shape of a ship emerged from the gloom. It was the Navy ship, the *Short Splice*, and she pulled astern. The *Short Splice* was not equipped for a rescue but was in radio contact with the Coast Guard. From across the seas, the officers of the *Short Splice* told the survivors of the *Fort Mercer* that cutters were on the way.

Then a second and a third and a fourth shape appeared. They were the cutters *Eastwind, Unimak,* and *Acushnet.* The *Eastwind* fired a line aboard the stern and passed over walkie-talkies. The plan was to evacuate the stern, if the men wanted to come off.

Bushnell, the chief engineer, took a loose command then. The stern was relatively stable. He thought they should stay on the stern and perhaps they could salvage the ship.

Those who wanted to stay could muster with him on the upper deck. Those who wanted to evacuate could go to the lower deck. Only three other men joined Bushnell on the upper deck. Below, thirty men voted with their feet to evacuate.

They may have demanded a recount when they watched the *Eastwind* for a while. She was pitching side to side in the big waves, far less stable it seemed than the stern section. In fact, this was due to the light ballast in the cutter. She was stable enough and seaworthy, but she rocked and rolled like a carnival ride.

Bushnell was unsure whether anyone should try to transverse the gap between the two ships. The plan was to rig a raft between the two ships and pull the raft over to the cutter.

A mild confrontation of sorts occurred then. C.W. Hindley was just the assistant cook, but he had been a combat marine and wanted to know what Bushnell thought. Hindley was disgusted at the lack of leadership and the panic on the boats. Never mind that Bushnell had been below, steering the stern out of the way of the bow. Bushnell was the senior officer. He should take charge. What was his assessment of the raft rescue, Hindley demanded.

And Bushnell said something like, "It's too hazardous."

And the cook shot back, saying essentially, "Well, isn't it hazardous staying here on a half-ship?"

"You want to be the first across?" Bushnell shot back.

"Yeah," the cook said. He wanted nothing more to do with Bushnell.

And so it was to be. Hindley stood on the rail of the stern. Bushnell had given him a hand-copied piece of paper with the names of all the men still alive. He stood on the rail and jumped the 30 feet down, trying to time it so he hit the small raft below.

He missed and was plunged into the churning seas. The cold of such water, as it always does, left him breathless. But the cook fought his way to the raft, grabbed it and hoisted himself in.

Then the *Eastwind* crew pulled on the lines and Ben Stabile, a gunnery officer on the *Unimak*, thought the whole scene resembled the Cyclone ride at Coney Island. The raft was twisting up and down, torqued this way and that by the sea, blown about, turned nearly upside down, corkscrewed through the air.

But the raft made it and so did the cook. He scrambled up a net alongside the ship and soon was onboard turning over the muster list to the captain of the *Eastwind*. Two more men made that trip.

Then, aboard the *Acushnet*, Lieutenant Commander John Joseph radioed to Captain Peterson aboard the *Eastwind*. The *Acushnet* was essentially a seagoing salvage tug. Joseph thought he had a plan that might work better. Would Peterson consider it?

It couldn't hurt to try, Peterson said, so they ceased the raft operation and let Joseph go to work.

He then brought the 213-foot ship in close to the stern section of the *Fort Mercer*. The men from above could see the big tug rise and fall with the wave cycles. One moment, the cutter would be 25 feet below deck; the next she would rise like an elevator with the waves and be right even with the deck of the half-ship.

And that is how they did it in the end. The men gathered on the stern, timed it just right, and just stepped across onto the *Acushnet*. It was simpler than disembarking at a regular port of call. It was that easy. Seven men went on the first pass, before the cycle of the sea dropped her. But the big tug neatly steered in again and more men scampered aboard, high and dry now. Eighteen in all made the passage and Stabile, staring on from the *Unimak*, thought the seamanship of Joseph among the most remarkable ever he had seen. The skipper had managed to come that close in horrendous seas, hold the ship steady and cause no damage to the cutter, the half-ship, any of his men, or any of the crew.

The stern section of the *Fort Mercer* with cutter standing by.

Bushnell, the chief engineer, meanwhile had convinced much of the rest of the crew that he could steer the *Fort Mercer* stern well enough to maintain headway and control against the waves. The Coast Guard was offering a tow, and the company had actually called salvage tugs. The rest of the men stayed on board with Bushnell and for all practical purposes the rescue was done. The *Fort Mercer* stern was not in the same fix as the *Pendleton*. The *Fort Mercer* was still far out to sea and the buoyancy, while not ideal, was strong. There was no danger of running aground.

As for the bow of the *Fort Mercer*? That was a completely different story.

Like the men on the bow of the *Pendleton*, the officers and crew on the bow section of the *Fort Mercer* seemed doomed.

The *Fort Mercer* bow turned ever more perpendicular to the sea. Paetzel and his men were thrown about the bridge and went crashing into each other and the sharp corners of instruments and machinery that were designed only for slow, deliberate movements. Water crested over the bridge and drenched them all and they clung to whatever they could to save their balance and their lives.

Paetzel ran down to his quarters to get drier clothes. He was soaked through. A huge sea washed through the half-ship then and filled his cabin. His own cabin was now a tank of water that he could not escape from. He was drowning in his own cabin.

Then, a moment later, the sea receded and dumped him on the floor. He was waterlogged, of course, and so were all the clothes in his cabin.

Worse than that, even, the sea had stripped him of his shoes and socks and all dignity. He was barefooted now as he trudged back up toward the bridge and to the relative safety there.

He took charge, then, as masters of ships are supposed to do. He would give the orders.

One good thing was, they were all calm. They were nine men: the captain, the chief mate, the second mate, and the third mate. They were Jack Brewer, Fahrner, and Vince Guilden, respectively. Ed Turner, the purser who paid the bills and was essentially an accountant, was there, as was John V. Reilly, the radioman; they knew he was a good man to have on the blinker lights. Then there was the quartermaster, Culver, and the two seamen who had just joined the bridge five minutes before the ship split. Perley W. Newman was an experienced able-bodied seaman; Jerome C. Higgins was a young kid, an ordinary seaman.

From the start, they looked after each other. Fahrner, the second officer, saw his drenched captain and dug out a blanket and offered it to him. Then Fahrner saw Higgins was without a life jacket. The kid had looked scared as he was coming up the catwalk before noon to take his shift. What lousy luck. Fahrner took off his own life jacket and gave it to the kid. Not to worry, he said, I'll find one.

The Fort Mercer stern, under steam.

Guilden, the third officer, told Fahrner that was just fine. Give away your life jacket. But you're wearing this. And Guilden passed him a length of line, a rope, and then tied it around Fahrner. The other end of the line was tied to Guilden who wore a life jacket. The theory was: We're lined together; you wash over, I wash over; both of us will float. All of this happened more or less without Paetzel having to give any orders.

Exactly what orders should Paetzel give? Who knew. Who knew how to captain a half-a-ship tilted at five degrees to starboard and forty-five degrees to the sea, with the bridge window pointed toward the quartered sky and seas washing through the doors?

They tried an SOS but the emergency batteries failed and the radio was dead.

"Open one door and keep it opened," Paetzel said. "The last thing we want to do is get trapped in here and drown." My God, he'd come close enough to that already today. Everyone agreed this was the right thing to do.

Then the captain shucked off the blanket and retrieved an old fur coat he kept on the bridge. It felt warmer. But all of them were going numb. He searched for anything to tie around his feet but found nothing. The winds ripped through the bridge; the spray and waves and rain and snow were relentless. The bridge itself was taking water so they moved into the closed chart room adjoining the bridge. They could look up and out and see their own bow high above them, relatively clear of the waves. Of course, that's where the buoyancy was. The fore tanks were empty, filled only with air. That's how they loaded to keep their draft high because of the stranding in the channel in Louisiana on the Mississippi. The mid-tanks were ruptured and flooded with water. So they floated bow-high.

They kept the stern section in sight for perhaps ten to fifteen minutes, twenty at the most. Then they were alone.

Six

CERTAIN DEATH

February 18, 1952
Chatham Lifesaving Station—12:15 p.m.

W hen he heard that the *Fort Mercer* split in two, Warrant Officer Cluff did some quiet calculations. True there were cutters heading toward the scene. But even if they got there, those big ships might not be able to maneuver in close to the tanker.

The lifeboats could. And if they made any sort of time through the storm, they could be there at the *Fort Mercer* in three or four hours, much faster than the cutters. But 36-foot lifeboats in 40-foot waves (some of them were peaking at 60, if the cutters could be believed), more than 25 miles out?

Cluff was the new guy and for the old guard Coasties like Masachi, he was too new and abandoned all traditons. Newcomb, the old commander, had a family in Chatham, but he did the same ten days on, two days off that his men did. His children would gather after school at the entrance to the Coast Guard station, hoping to catch a glimpse of their dad. But their dad would not go out to meet them. For the ten days on, his kids were all the Coasties inside the building. He would do benevolent prowls about the facility, puffing on his smelly pipe to let the Coast Guard kids know he was coming. Forewarned by the pipe, the Coasties would stop whatever they were doing wrong and start doing what they were supposed to be doing. And at that point, Newcomb would instruct them in a gentle collegial way. A modern business school tract might have dubbed it "management by walking around" or "catching them doing right." Newcomb knew it instinctively and through his technique passed on Coast Guard culture. The men admired him.

No, they loved him. There was a direct connection between Newcomb and the old Lifesaving Service guys—the ones who would live for months at a time in beach houses in the company of men and a culture of courage. He was far, far more like family, more like a big brother or a father than a "manager."

But Newcomb had been promoted and Cluff was … well, more modern. More a corporate modern manager. He lived in Chatham and slept at home each night. When storms came, he was known to leave the lifeboat compound to drive by his house and check on his television antennae, one of the early ones sprouting on Chatham roofs.

And if this change of culture for the men was not enough, Cluff literally seemed to speak a different language. Many of the Coasties were Massachusetts born and bred, with a clipped Massachusetts diction. Cluff was Virginia all the way and at times the men honestly looked at him blank-faced when he gave orders. They sincerely did not understand him.

It was not long before Masachi bristled under Cluff's command, and soon he was gone, promoted and gone up and out to a cutter. But then Cluff brought in Boatswain's Mate Bangs to replace Masachi as number two. Bangs was Masachi with a sense of humor. He was demanding, but he could chuckle about his demands. And soon, Webber included, the men came to like Cluff and Bangs. Not like Newcomb and Masachi, but the looser approach had something going for it. It was good to be able to sneak off base for a few hours during your ten days on. It was good to know you could drive over and see your young wife when she was sick.

Looser did not mean sloppier in tough times like this, though, and now, Cluff had to make some hard decisions. He looked at his men; he looked at his boats. He turned to his best crew, his number two in the command structure. Chief Bangs, he said, pick a crew and go out to the stern section of the *Fort Mercer*. Take the CG 36580. Run her out of Stage Harbor. You'll never make the Chatham Bar. And God bless.

When he saw Bangs go out, Webber thought, *My God, do they really think a lifeboat could actually make it that far out to sea in this storm? If the crew didn't freeze to death first, how would they be able to get the men off?* Webber saw the men leave around 1 p.m. and in his mind said goodbye to each one of his friends. He thought there was a good chance he would never see them alive again.

Cluff turned to Webber and dispatched him to round up more fishing vessels. Many more of them had broken loose in the storm. It was cold work but he welcomed it. The torque of the CG 36500 pulled a parade of small boats back to their moorings. It was past 3 p.m. when he had completed that work. He should call Miriam, he knew, but instead he stood near the radio room and the operations room, trying to follow the storm, wondering if his friend Bangs could possibly make it. He couldn't see how.

How could you send 36-foot boats into 40-foot waves? The boats were unsinkable, but not the men. The 125-foot cutters had come in, the seas were so rough. Even the bigger cutters were taking a beating out there. How could they send Bangs to his death?

Seven

CHAOS AND ORDER

February 18, 1952
Aboard the *Pendleton,* bow and stern

For the officers and seamen on the *Pendleton*, life fell apart nearly as quickly as the ship had. One moment, they were on watch, warm and in control. Within minutes, they were thrown against each other by the pitching seas, tilted at forty-five degrees to the surface of the ocean—if the surface of the ocean could be defined, for it was a mass of heaving waves.

It was not unknown for men to be rescued from the bows of splintered tankers. This was what Eugene Ericksen had witnessed five years earlier on the SS *Sacketts Harbor*, a T-2 cruising peacefully en route to Alaska in a cold but calm sea in 1947.

He was on watch near the stern at around 1 a.m., embroidering the war stories he told now in peacetime, when he heard a thunderous crack and felt the ship rise up gently as if she had nosed over a speed bump. All the lights went out.

"We've *hit* something," he thought, but knew that was improbable and began running toward the bow of the ship.

Then, at midship, he grabbed the rail and came skittering to a halt. The ship simply ended. With no warning, in quiet waters, she had split in two.

His half of the *Sacketts Harbor*, the stern half, floated evenly and seemed almost stable. But in front of Ericksen, the bow section of the *Sacketts Harbor* bobbed at a crazy angle. He could see the officers hanging on to slanted decks. He could see the whole cross section of the ship as if it were the cutaway view of a dollhouse. They were hanging on madly to anything they could on the bow, as it bobbed and bucked, twisting to that same forty-five-degree angle in the water.

The Navy, thank God, was right there and pulled those men off quickly in the quiet waters of the Pacific, but Ericksen did not think the officers in the bow would have stood much of a chance if the destroyer had not been right there and seen it happening. For starters, the officers in the bow had the radios but no power. And the stern had the power but no radios. They would have had no way to get the word out. And if there had been any sea at all? He was fine in the stern section; the officers would have been toast.

And on board the *Pendleton*, they were—or nearly so. Visibility was a few feet as spray, snow, sleet, and rain pounded them. Green water—heavy-duty waves—crashed through the bridge. Yes, there was an emergency power source for the radio, as Chief Engineer Sybert, in the stern, had thought. But no, there was no chance, no chance at all, to send out an SOS. The officers, the radioman, the ABs who had stayed behind at the shift change were thrown around like rag dolls.

Most of them were trapped in the bridge or down below. The fore tanks of the bow were empty and buoyant so the aft of the new half-ship plunged downward at an acute angle. So they were at best poorly protected against battering seas; at worst, they were exposed to them wholly, dunked down into the cold ocean repeatedly.

Even those who were able to cling to something solid and stay aboard the ship found little future or hope. They were not prepared for this and were not wearing heavy clothing, having been safe and sound in sheltered, warmed spaces. Wet, cold, and whipped by 50–mile per hour winds, the officers and seamen were in peril of hypothermia. Exposure could claim lives in minutes under these conditions.

Still, they fought it. Fitzgerald, the captain; Martin Moe, the chief mate; Joseph W. Colgan, the second mate; Harold Bancus, the third mate; James G. Greer, the radioman; Joseph L. Landry, an able-bodied seaman; Herman G. Gatlin, also an AB; and Bill Roy Morgan, an ordinary seaman: they fought it with everything they had.

By contrast, life on the stern section of the *Pendleton* was almost calm, a broken half-ship under the command of a chief engineer and an able seaman. Order and routine of a sense had returned to the stern section—not that any of this was routine.

Hicks and Steele, with Sybert's agreement, decided to post two-man watches. The two seamen would stay alert for passing ships or planes or signals from afar. They also would watch for land—for the Nauset and Chatham coastlines they knew could not be too far away.

Without being told, the cooks and mess men fired up a big kettle of boiling water and poured dozens of eggs in to cook. This wasn't comfort food—not like a hot bubbling bowl of soup. But the food was portable protein. A big kettle of coffee bubbled constantly, and the seamen and engineers would pop in, grab a few eggs and a cup of coffee, and chat. Or they'd pop a half dozen eggs in their pockets both to keep warm and "fueled."

None of them stayed below for long, though. Most of them instinctively crowded toward the top of the ship, and there, in a passageway that was sheltered, passed the time, exchanging stories, speculating on where the rescuers were, listening to the repeated danger signals that Tiny Myers blew, hour after hour.

Much of the talk was about launching the boats—and how impossible that seemed. Much of the talk, too, was what happened if the ship ran aground. Would she turn turtle then, dumping them into still-deep water too far from shore? This was the story of most shipwrecks along the coast. The ships ran aground in water that was too shallow for ships but still deep enough to drown humans. Huge surfs and currents would rip the shore.

Hicks and Steele actually had been able to rig auxiliary manual steering in the engine room. They had a "wheel" to steer the rudder. And Sybert could maneuver using the single propeller as well. The good parts of the T-2 were working well. It was nice to have that electrical power and the ability to steam aft when needed.

But this half-ship was not the same as having a whole ship. The control was tentative at best, downright hazardous at worst. The water got rougher as they neared the shore and the ship bucked and heaved more, slamming down hard on its new, open bow. This new half-ship looked more like the stub of cigar than a sleek panatela. There were no "lines" left to part waters or funnel waves aside.

And the men on top needed to be careful. Green water, the waves that were more of the sea than of any wave peak, would cover the decks.

One man would stand aft, one man would stand forward. That way they could keep an eye on each other and look out to the sea and up to the sky. And none would grow too cold or too exposed on half-hour watches.

In one sense, Sybert and the seamen Hicks and Steele had taken control of the situation. In another sense, they seemed to just channel order. None of the men on the *Pendleton* seemed to panic. There was no rush to the boats. They followed orders. In another sense, they seemed to act as one.

But it was all getting old and cold after a while.

Help was coming, they thought at first. The SOS had gone out from the bow.

Then an hour passed, and another. Two hours passed and then two more. Then four more hours had passed. Ten hours in all, twenty two-man shifts—and nothing.

It was around 2 p.m., nearly eight hours after he started hauling on the whistle, that Tiny Myers blew the distress call and someone outside the ship actually heard it.

In Chatham, on land, snug indoors against the nor'easter, Joe Nickerson, a carpenter, thought he heard a noise mixed in with the wind, a noise that did not belong to the storm. Outdoors, he cocked his head and listened again. The noise grew stronger. It was a ship's whistle. It would blow four times, then stop, blow four times, then stop.

Nickerson sped to Fire Chief George Goodspeed's home and reported the distress call. The two men raced to the Coast Guard station with the news. There, they found Bill Woodsman, the radar man, looking intently at his screen.

None of them realized it at the time, but they had discovered the wreck of the *Pendleton*, nearly ten hours after she had split in two. The radar man reported to Cluff. We have two tankers down, he said.

Actually, if you looked at the situation, it was even worse than that. They had four ships down, not two. The little Coast Guard station had gone from one ship, the *Fort Mercer*, in possible trouble to four half-ships in dire trouble.

Webber sucked in his breath. He was watching Cluff closely. What to do? What to do? Finally, Cluff made his move. He radioed Bangs. Head for the *Pendleton*, he told him. Forget the *Fort Mercer* for now. The cutters can get her. Come back for the *Pendleton*.

"You," Cluff told Webber. "I want you to head down the beach on land and see if you can get a line to the *Pendleton*."

Webber exhaled. For a moment, he thought Cluff was going to send him out in a boat.

Eight

PING-PONG

February 18, 1952
With Chief Bangs

At 12:30 p.m., Bangs and his crew had launched to rescue the *Fort Mercer* and found that the lifeboat's radio transmitter was only half working. Bangs could hear fine but could say nothing. He headed toward Monomoy on his way to the *Fort Mercer* and stopped at the *Pollock Rip* lightship to check in and tell the station he could only receive.

There he received new orders. Head for the bow of the *Pendleton*. There were two wrecks now, and he was needed at the bow of the *Pendleton*.

The seas were overwhelming. In a 36-foot lifeboat, Bangs and his crew faced 40-foot waves. Cutters, merchant ships, and the lightships themselves were having difficulty maintaining stability in such a storm. The 125-foot cutters had turned back.

But the little boat cut through the spray, the foam, and the monstrous swells, climbing up the slope of one wave like a cog railroad engine, then slushing down the wall of the wave like a speed skier.

A mile on, just as they said, there she was: the bow of the *Pendleton*. Tilted and rocking, bow pointing skyward, bridge awash in green water, the bow rocked and twisted still.

Bangs came in close. He sounded his Klaxon constantly. He completely circled the ship. There was no sign of life, no lights. But to be sure, he circled again, Klaxon wailing, hailing anyone on board to signal back.

He paused, assessed the situation, made one last pass in close and concluded no one had survived. The bow was perilously close to the shore now. Waves were breaking over the bridge, and there was nothing more he could do. He returned to the *Pollock*, back across the hills of sea.

Head to the *stern* of the *Pendleton*, he was ordered by Cluff. The *Fort Mercer* was in trouble but was farther out to sea. She would drift clear of Cape Cod but the *Pendleton* stern was on a drift line that would carry her into the surf.

Bangs prepared to set out for the stern of the *Pendleton*. But as he did, more news came. The *McCulloch*, a cutter that could not get in close to the bow because of shallow water, was close enough to spot lights and life on the bow of the *Pendleton*. The CG 36850 had apparently roused a survivor. But he had not made it to the bridge in time for the small boat to see him.

So Bangs now turned his little boat back through the same wild waters he had transited twice before. He and his crew were soaked to the bone and growing ever more hypothermic themselves. Still, they bore down on the *Pendleton* again.

And yes! You could see him. It had been 1700 hours the first time they circled the bow, and there was still some light. Now it was 7 p.m. and dark. The *McCulloch* was circling near the bow. She was pumping over oil—a practice of the time intended to calm the seas. Bangs put his spotlight up on the starboard side of the *Pendleton* bridge and there the man was. The *McCulloch* had him spotlighted as well.

A lone figure at the railing on the wing of the bridge was yelling to them. They could hear his voice—could at least hear there *was* a voice—but could not understand the words. They thought he said he was the last man, the only one left. They could not make out his face and did not know who he was.

But they could get him. They knew they could. It was not impossible if they timed it correctly. Bangs had line-throwing equipment and other tools of rescue. He wanted to get in very close, to find out for sure how many men there were to be rescued and not do this in a slip-shod manner. Quick movements now could cost lives, not save them. This is when you had to be coolest.

Just then, a great curl of water rose from behind the *Pendleton* bow and swept through the bridge and over the deck. It came from behind the man after covering the bridge. The man on the rail was caught up from behind by the wave and was carried forward by it.

He held on. He was on the outside of the ship now—on the wrong, ocean side of the rail—but he held on a long time. Then he seemed no longer able to keep his grip. And as his grip lessened, he leapt with all his might out from the ship, toward Bangs and the rescuers.

And Bangs headed straight for him. It was dark. But the man landed only a boat length away, just 30 to 40 feet away. The crew picked him up in their spotlight and crept toward him for the rescue.

From behind them, a sea the size of a house rose up and carried the boat and crew forward. The CG 36850, more buoyant than the man in the water, ran faster with the sea. So when the men next looked, the man was now several boat lengths behind them.

Bangs did not waste time. He kept the spotlight steadily on the man and backed the boat toward him. They were closer than before now, less than a boat length. He was not going to turn-to and lose sight of the man. That was the important thing: keep him in sight, in the spotlight.

At just 20 feet away, they threw him a line. And again the sea rose and carried them, farther this time than the last time. The searchlight stayed on the man, then lost him, found him, lost him, found him.

Bangs thought he saw the life jacket, then lost it. Then he thought he saw it, but could not confirm it. Back and forth, they ploughed the waters, trying to fix where he was, where they were, all in a swirl of waves, eddies, cross currents, ripping winds, snow, sleet, and spray in the dead of night.

They searched for more than an hour. The *McCulloch* could not come closer for fear of running aground. Bangs looked up at the bridge and saw that for the most part, it was completely immersed.

He returned to the lightship and there, he fastened a line on and rode out the night. The conditions at Pollock Rip were nearly impassable. He and his crew had tried valiantly to save seamen from three half-ships— but they could no more that night.

For a Coastie, there was no worse feeling.

Nine

ORDERS

February 18, 1952
With Webber

A strange procession of vehicles crawled out from Chatham toward Nauset Inlet. A DUKW and a Dodge four-wheel drive "power wagon" moved over the slippery beaches, buffeted by spray and wind.

They soon came up to where the *Pendleton* stern ought to be, but they saw nothing. They were near Nauset Beach, above the Mayo's Duck Farm, atop a hill.

Then for a moment, the blow broke and the snow and drizzle slackened. Through that hole in the weather, Webber could see the ghostly outline of the stern of the *Pendleton*. She was huge, even a quarter mile offshore. He thought she looked as if she were galloping along the huge waves, dark and sinister. The stern sent up froth and foam each time it rose and fell in the seas.

Through the wind they could hear a whistle—Tiny Myers and his crewmen, pulling down on the lanyard. Four blasts and then a pause. Four short blasts and then a pause.

Webber could not answer them. There was no way he could shoot a line to them at that distance in these winds, no chance of a rescue via line and trolley using the old Lyle Gun and the "Breeches Buoy" method.

They did not even have a radio. The best thing they could do was get back to the Coast Guard station fast. They slipped and slid back to Chatham to confirm the sighting. And Webber could hear how it was all shaping up on the radio once he got there. He heard how Bangs and his boat were like a ping-pong ball. Deployed here to the *Fort Mercer*, there to the *Pendleton* bow, here to the *Pendleton* stern, then back to the *Pendleton* bow.

And there grew in him a sickening feeling. Up until now, he has worried about his friends out there in the boat. But now he knew what was coming his way. Cluff had no one for the *Pendleton* stern. Cluff was delaying it, but Webber knew this assignment was coming his way.

He *knew* what Cluff was thinking. They arrived back at the station dripping wet and told Cluff what they had seen. Cluff was silent for minutes. And then Cluff—knowing he was almost certainly pronouncing a death sentence for the young man—said slowly in his Virginia accent, "Webber, pick yourself a crew. Ya-all got to take the 36500 out over the bar and assist that thar ship, ya-heah?"

Webber heard all right, and a sinking feeling came to his stomach. *No chance at the Chatham Bar. No chance! And why me? Why me? My wife is sick. I haven't spoken to her in two days. Why me?* Instead, Webber said, "Yes sir, Mr. Cluff, I'll get ready."

Bernie Webber knew exactly who he wanted for the crew: all men he had worked with before. The only problem was, none of them were there. There wasn't even a full crew left in the station. Just a junior engineer, one seaman, and a guy from a lightship who was in transit, waiting for the storm to break to go out to his ship. He wasn't even a rescue guy. That was another reason not to go, another reason the mission was impossible. He could tell Cluff that.

69

"Hey Webb," said Seaman Richard Livesey. "I'll go out with you if you want." Engineman Andrew J. Fitzgerald and Irving Maske, the lightship guy, offered the same deal: Bernie, if you need us, we'll go.

Well, hell. He knew Livesey. A funny guy. People sometimes didn't take him that seriously around the station because he was always joking, but Webber had seen him in action and knew he was a good man. He had this odd habit, a humble one, forget about the jokes and stuff. Whenever they finished a patrol when Livesey was on board, no matter how trivial or routine, Livesey would have a single parting phrase to Bernie. "Thanks, Webb," he would say quietly. And there was no hint of a joke in it, no irony. Livesey was a good man. He got excited and enthusiastic, even if they were running supplies to a lighthouse.

And the other guys? Well, he didn't know the lightship guy at all, except that he cooked for them sometimes—and he was pretty good. He knew Fitzgerald was first-rate.

Not his regular crew. But they were willing. They were able. He would be lying if he used them as an excuse not to go out.

Solemnly, Webber led his little band of volunteers out to the CG 36500 mooring. Along the way a friend and neighbor, a veteran fishermen named John Stello, hailed Webber. Stello had a reputation as a fearless risk taker—a man who went out anywhere there were fish, any time, in any weather.

"You guys going out in *this*?" Stello looked worried. Webber nodded grimly.

"You guys better get … *lost* … before you get too far out," Stello said. In other words, say you gave it a try, then come back.

This was about as official a cultural permission to play it safe as Bernie could get. The roughest toughest fisherman in a tough fishing community was telling him to take a dive, to hit the canvas and stay down. There would be no goading slurs if Bernie did that.

"Call Miriam," Webber bellowed back. Let my wife know what's up. In so many words: tell her how I died.

Stello thought about that one. The upside of making that call. Tell Miriam now? Let her know she's a widow, or about to be? Or give her a few more hours thinking her husband might be alive and well. He did not tell Webber yes or no about that one. Miriam knew how it worked on nights like this, that there was always a chance her husband was at risk. Stello would have to give it some thought. Webber knew he'd do the right thing. They were both men of the sea, and he knew Stello would see that Miriam learned of his fate appropriately and would handle it the right way.

For Webber, Chatham was like a snow globe with him inside it: a village with small cottages and glowing lights that showed through the snow. He loved this place. It was magical.

They rowed out in the dory with no problems and clambered on the CG 36500. The ninety-horsepower motor sputtered and spat and Webber steered it from the aft-most position. One could ski behind a ninety-horsepower engine attached to a normal boat but that was not the job of a lifeboat. The job of a lifeboat was to get there and back, carrying a load slowly and surely.

Well, Webber thought, given everything, this is the boat I want. I could not ask for anything better. And I know the bar as well as anyone. Cluff's choice made sense for a moment.

Then they were heading at eight knots through the protected harbor, already soaked to the skin and shivering, facing darkness broken only by the white of the blizzard. The shore looked like a Christmas card—lights of houses soft through the snow, blurry harbor lights.

Webber keyed the radio mike and checked in. His confidence had waivered. He was positive they would receive orders to return.

"Proceed as directed," the radio crackled. And in the dark, with the lights of the town of Chatham muffled by the blizzard, the young men did an odd thing. One of them began humming an old hymn, someone picked up the words and they all began singing. Webber did not even recall knowing the words before then.

Rock of ages, cleft for me,
Let me hide thyself in thee;
Let the water and the blood,
From thy wounded side which flowed,
Be of sin the double cure,
Save from wrath and make pure.

The religious solemnity of the hymn then gave way to a more sentimental, secular tune. "Harbor Lights" had been a huge hit in 1950. Now, the young men sang the verses they remembered.

I saw the harbor lights
They only told me we were parting
The same old harbor lights that once brought you to me
I watched the harbor lights
How could I help if tears were starting
Goodbye to tender nights beside the silv'ry sea.

Neither song was a real upper. Not exactly the "Flight of the Valkyries." But both were authentic of the feelings aboard the boat. The songs comforted the men.

The CG 36500 reached Morris Island and now they could hear the water roaring on Chatham Bar. Webber called in again, thinking, *Come on, come on, recall us, return to base. This is impossible.*

"Imperative you continue to sea," the radio crackled back. They could not see the waves ahead but could hear the crash and bang ripple down the shore in front of them. The noise was fearsome. Breakers of this sort sound as if a thousand forklift trucks are dropping a thousand loads of lumber in succession from a great height.

Webber maneuvered the little boat closer, into the vortex of the noise. Still they could not see the waves, only hear the explosion of thundering surf. Could they make it? Hell no, they couldn't make it.

Stand at the seashore as the breakers hit your ankles, or your knees. Catch a 3-foot one at your waist and feel that force. Take a 4-foot breaker at your chest. Then imagine monster breakers twice your size, some three-times your size, tall as a house and hammering hard on the sand, pounding the sand and tons heavy. Not a hammer coming down, but the anvil. This is what they faced. Anyone could *see* they couldn't make it. The boat would be thrown back by tons of water, smashed to splinters on the sand with the men inside.

And Webber thought: no one will blame us if we turn back. I'll just tell them we couldn't make it. Everyone heard what Stello said and he's one of the toughest fishermen about. No one would criticize him. Stello had given him the code words. Bernie knew it was a pass from the culture. No goading slurs here. All Bernie had to do was say they were lost, they could not get their bearings.

Webber's whole body shivered and did not stop. Take it a step further, he said to himself. Suppose we survive the bar? He only had a magnetic compass, no radar. They'd never find the ship. There probably weren't any survivors on the stern. Even if he did risk the lives of his crew to cross the bar, this would be senseless. They'd never find the *Pendleton*.

He would turn back now. Why waste the lives of these good men on his boat. He was responsible for three souls here. He knew they were looking at him for leadership now, out of the corners of their eyes. They were hoping they'd turn back, too.

Then he thought: Who am I? What's my job? The question came to him in a calm way and the answer came in the same manner with great clarity. *I am a Coast Guard first class boatswain mate … My job is the sea and to save those in peril upon it.*

And the tradition of the Coast Guard, the pure simple heroic tradition of saving lives, the tradition and the "book" propelled Webber. Every Coast Guardsmen who had trained him, encouraged him, and drilled this tradition into him. Every man who trained the men who trained him. Every one of them was there with him. The *Landry*, Newcomb,

Masachi, the old guy at the light tower, Bangs, Cluff. All the way back to Pea Island and the lifesavers who coined the phrase. All the way back to Etheridge.

You have to go out. You do not have to come back.

Webber keyed the mike. "We'll try," he said.

He still could not see the bar. He could only hear it, feel it. He did not sense any heroic spirit. No bravado. He felt resigned. He was like a soldier ordered into battle, into a hopeless charge. He had his orders. He had his discipline. Now he would die.

He was harnessed into the boat by a rig that lashed him to the wheel. His men had no harnesses. They all crowded into the coxswain's partition behind the windshield. Webber alone wore no life jacket, as it restricted his ability to steer. Well, at least they'll find their bodies, he thought.

"*Hang on!*" Webber yelled to his crew and then gunned the engine. The CG 36500 turned at full speed into the darkness, into the vortex of the horrible, growling Chatham Bar.

The first wave seized the CG 36500 with no respect at all for its ton of bronze. It flipped the boat, her ballast, and all four men completely clear of the water—just as if she were a flimsy balsa wood model—and flung her back toward the harbor.

They were airborne, hanging there above the monster waves, clear of the water, a part of the snowy blizzard and the air now, little prop speeding, whining, clear of the water, biting only air. The hang time seemed an eternity.

Then they hammered down hard in the trough of the wave, hard on the boat's side. They were far, far over on their side. Too far over. Webber struggled in the rear to turn the bow into the next monster, to try to meet it head on.

They were not going to make it. Already, the curl of the breaker hung above the boat, and the base of the wave too was crashing, crushing down on CG 36500.

Ten

STRANDED

February 18–19, 1952
Aboard the bow of the *Fort Mercer*

In the chart room of the bow section of the *Fort Mercer*, the general alarm—a Klaxon-like siren—continued to sound, powered by the emergency batteries on board the bow. None of the men seemed to notice the annoying noise. It was just a part of the chaos. Then Fahrner, the second officer, snapped the alarm switch off. The general alarm was loud enough to let men on board the ship know there was a problem, but not loud enough to serve as any sort of "rescue-us" signal to searchers.

The officers took stock. They had no food, no radio, no water, no flares. What they did have was a blinker light to communicate to any ships that came near. In the stern section, the blinker would have done no one any good. No one aft knew code. The officers were engineers, and only the deck officers and the radioman—"Sparks," as he was called on every ship—could blink Morse code. It was terribly old-fashioned even then, but it was the most modern technology the men on the bow possessed.

And soon, they would have a chance to use it. Out of the gloom, they saw ship lights. It had been hours since the wreck. Out of the gloom and the spits of snow and foam and rain sailed the *Short Splice*, a Navy utility ship. And it was blinking out rapid code to them—a series of dots and dashes via its blinker—about 5 p.m.

For Fahrner, it was a joy to see Sparks and the chief mate work their battery-powered blinker, which was little more than a flashlight. Geez, these guys were pros. Fahrner knew some code but Sparks and the mate? It was as if Fahrner spoke high school French and these guys were Parisians.

A burst of blinks, of dashes and dots of electronic light, would flash from the gray shadow of the Navy ship and Sparks would translate.

This is the Navy ship *Short Splice*.

The chief would flash back a detailed report of their status. No food, warmth, or water. Fear capsizing. Help?

No good for us to try, the *Short Splice* winked back. We're not equipped for rescue. But Coast Guard cutters are on the way. A boat is on the way. Estimated time of arrival is three hours for the Coast Guard. Hang in there. We'll stand by.

A cheer and groan rose within the men on the bow. Help was on the way. This was good. You couldn't argue with that.

But three hours to wait? It was cold and getting colder. Hypothermia and frostbite were taking their tolls. The men could not remain functional for much longer. It had been nearly five hours and most of them were drenched. They'd try putting their hands in their pockets in their pants to warm up their fingers and restore feeling to them. It would work for a while, but even in their pockets their hands grew colder—a sure sign their overall body temperature was dropping. Captain Paetzel was still without shoes or boots and his feet were frostbitten pegs with little feeling in them.

It was 5 p.m. and light was fading. So the rescue ships, when they arrived, would be approaching in the dark.

Still, they were glad to see her when she arrived. The cutter *Yakutat*, with Commander Joseph W. Naab on the bridge, beat the *Short Splice* estimate by about half an hour and came into sight, well lit, around 7:30 p.m.

Fahrner could not keep track of the code as it flashed between the two ships. It went something like this.

This is the Coast Guard cutter *Yakutat*. What is your situation?

Sparks and the chief let them know.

Dots and dashes flashed back between the cutter and the half-ship and the short version of the long message from the cutter was this. We're going to fire lines to you. Then we'll take you off using trolleys, or haul you off with rafts. Stay inside as we shoot the lines.

Soon, there were muffled explosions from the cutter as their line cannons detonated and shot out lead-laced lines to the *Fort Mercer*.

Seven times they fired. They tried all angles, gauging the wind, the seas, and the snow as best they could. Seven times, the spray and wind carried off the lines; none landed.

The eighth time seemed the charm. The line passed over the *Fort Mercer* bow section and stayed there. Problem was, it landed in the radio antennae above the bridge house. The men on the bow could see it and they set out to retrieve it.

Huge waves! Winds of 50 miles per hour and more. Three times they set out to retrieve the line. Three times they were driven back. It was just too dangerous. Water was sweeping the bridge housing. The bow was listing more to starboard now as well. The bow had the floating action of a bottom-weighted fishing bobber. The front of the bow section and its empty tanks floated free of the fray, for the most part, above the deck-house, which was regularly dunked and drenched by the sea.

This was a heartbreaking business for Naab. He was meant to save men's lives. That was his duty. But he could not put a single line aboard. He could see that the men would not last much longer where they were.

And so it was the officers of the *Yakutat* blinkered over the question: Can you make it to the forward-most bow area? You'll have better protection there. And we'll have better access to you. Forget about us shooting lines in this dark soupy weather. We'll float some lighted rafts down to you. But you have to get out of the bridge and down to the rail level some how.

Great idea. How?

There was no longer any interior passage. Go down the stairs to the main deck? The passageways were flooded, just as the captain's quarters had been. The exterior ladders had been ripped loose and carried away by the waves.

If they had some rope, they might make it out the bridge windows or off the deck or out the portal on the side where the wind was not so hard.

If they had a rope. Might as well say, if they had a helicopter. Better yet, wings. They had neither rope nor helicopter. No wings either.

And Culver, the quartermaster, said, guys, let's tie the blankets together. It was like the classic escape caper where one ties sheets and blankets together and shinnies to the ground from a third-floor window.

Fahrner thought about that. He fingered the blankets. They would have to rip them and tie them. He doubted they would hold up—particularly for Paetzel, who was a heavy guy.

Fahrner fished out the signal flags from the bridge. These were the lines and the flags that were run up the mast to show various states of the ship or the weather. They were tough cords, tough flags. They could use them instead of the blankets.

Everyone agreed in an instant and they set about to work. The chief and Sparks blinkered back the plan. All of them were happy to be doing something, and doing something they knew: knots and lines were a primary skill of seamen. All of them, captain through the ordinary seamen, set to work on forming this makeshift line.

A half hour later when they were finished, it seemed strong. And aboard the *Yakutat*, the rescuers were busy tying their own knots and lines. This was a makeshift effort they were assembling: a line of rafts, lighted, tied together by lines that were also lighted. They would use almost every piece of rope and line onboard the *Yak* to assemble the rescue apparatus.

If the men reached the deck level, the *Yakutat* would drift this line of rafts in close to them. The men could jump and swim to the rafts and lines. Or if they were lucky, if the drift was right, they could jump into the rafts. That is, if the men reached the deck level. If the signal line rope held.

It was well past 9 p.m. in the evening and the storm was not slackening. The men had been exposed now for more than nine hours to freezing temperatures and raking, wet winds.

Fahrner looked down the side of the bridge house. It was a long drop down to a catwalk that led forward. Peering through the spray, he could see there were four grids missing on the catwalk. He rethought the entire idea.

It was so cold, but he had no choice. It was the last thing to do, and that is how he saw it: the last thing to do, no choice now. They would die on that bridge—slowly by exposure or quickly by drowning. The starboard list was greater now. The bow section was tilted up but increasingly tilted over. By this time, their counterparts on the *Pendleton* bow were dead. Fahrner did not know that, but the *Yakutat* officers almost certainly did.

The chief mate, Jack Brewer, was the first man down the rope. He moved through a large porthole on the bridge, dangled for a moment, and went down the line. Waves nipped at his heels, but his feet caught the catwalk and he was down. Perfect.

This gave Fahrner strength and hope. He took the line that lashed him to the third mate and removed it. And without a life jacket, he too went down the line of cord and flags.

His legs flailed out for the catwalk. They caught. He gained purchase. He was down. And then he was moving forward. Forward and up. No time to stay and help the next man down. You had to hurry forward, scurry over those missing grids or the waves would catch you.

Third down was the third mate, and Guilden too made it and rushed to Fahrner. They reattached the line that bound them together. Both men were high up on the bow now and looked down the ramped deck of the *Fort Mercer* toward the bobbing bridge house. Then they opened the carpentry shed on the bow and began looking for a life jacket for Fahrner—and anything else dry that could keep them warm.

And so the men descended from the bridge to the main deck level. Paetzel and the radioman were the last two left. Paetzel was big, with a comfortable layer of fat to keep him warm. Sparks was very thin with no insulation from the cold. Still it was hard to tell who was shivering the hardest.

"Captain I'm not going to make it," Sparks said to Paetzel.

"You'll make it!" Paetzel replied. "Hold on until you reach the catwalk."

Sparks climbed through the porthole and hung onto the metal of the porthole for a long time before grabbing the line. He stared down at the catwalk, trying to time the waves. The wave cycles were perhaps 30 to 40 feet apart, and the timing needed to be right.

Down the line Sparks went. He saw a lull in the waves and descended toward the catwalk. The wave cycle was right. But he missed the catwalk with his legs. He landed on the deck itself with no purchase, no leverage, no point to catch himself. He flailed on the rope as the wave cycle, which had receded, built again and blew up a big monster that washed over him and the catwalk.

And Paetzel could see it all happen from above. He could see that Sparks held onto that line for a good long time before the sea just took him and washed him off to his death.

Paetzel did not waste time or second-guess his own descent. Death was certain in the bridge house. He ducked out through the portal, swung his considerable weight over onto the side of the ship, and nimbly enough for an overweight, out-of-shape old seadog with frostbitten feet, he caught the catwalk and moved forward.

What the men saw then was both phantasmagoric and utterly beautiful. The cutter had pulled upwind of the *Fort Mercer* bow. The *Yakutat* rescuers had tied a string of well-lit rafts together and floated them down from windward. All of this in a roaring blizzard in the dark of night.

The rafts drifted down, lights glowing through the snow, like someone's fantasy of a Christmas procession. On the forecastle, the men had a chance now to strike out for the rafts in the water. The *Yakutat* had said to jump when the rafts got close.

Fahrner and Guilden were in the forecastle carpentry shop rummaging for a life jacket. Fahrner found one and the two officers, literally bound together, undid the line between them. Paetzel was maneuvering up the tricky catwalk. And the chief mate and the two seamen looked at the line of rafts, the rescue processional. Up above, Coast Guard planes dropped flares. Lights cut through the motes of snow and rain. And down drifted the rafts toward them, even with the bow now.

Was this close enough? How far away were they? When should they jump?

Aboard the *Yakutat*, Naab watched with utter dread. They had been positioning the rafts to drift alongside the bow section, to get the rafts in close. This was easier said than done. The winds, the waves, the snow and rain all made it difficult to maneuver and drift the line down in the dark.

And at precisely the wrong moment, the line to the rafts gave way. Just parted and let the rescue processional loose into the storm.

The rafts swooped sharply toward the bow section. Naab did not even have time to warn the seamen. The cutter crew watched in horror, each of them thinking some version of, "Don't jump."

The chief mate and the seamen figured this was it. The line of rafts raced toward the bow section and came even with it. It was now or never. They did not hesitate. They had seen Sparks washed to his death. All three men climbed the railing of the *Fort Mercer* bow and jumped for the rafts. Only Higgins, the ordinary seaman, held back.

Paetzel and Fahrner met at the forecastle. Where's the chief and the other men? They asked each other the same question because none of them had seen the men jump. Only Higgins was left. They jumped, he told them.

Fahrner looked out at the rafts. Did they make it? No way. No way they could have, he thought. The rafts to his eye were 300 yards away across an expanse of mountainous seas. You've got five minutes in these waters, he figured. Five minutes before you would either drown or succumb to hypothermia.

As if to confirm it all, the rafts were quickly swept away and with them went every piece of line and equipment the *Yakutat* carried. So the cutter chased after her runaway rafts. The rescuers needed that equipment and there was always a chance, too. Always a chance that one of the men had made it, climbed into the raft, was riding out the waves now.

It took the *Yakutat* the better part of two hours to recover her gear. All this time, the men on the bow hunkered down, finding whatever warmth they could. The top of the bow was more stable, but it was not warmer. Paetzel found a flag and draped it over his head. His feet were still shoeless. The men took turns rubbing his feet, trying to keep the blood circulating there.

But increasingly the men felt hopeless. The chief and the radioman were both gone now—their aces on the blinker and code. There was little they could say now to the cutter and less they could understand as to the cutter's intention.

The *Yakutat* rounded in the water, her gear secure, and headed back to the bow of the *Fort Mercer*. She got as close as she could. The thought may have been to hail the survivors via loudspeaker, tell them the cutter would stand off until morning.

Higgins interpreted it as another rescue effort. The cutter seemed convincingly close. He jumped the rail and leapt for the cutter, falling into the chaos of ocean between the ship and the half-ship. He was gone in ten seconds. No one had a chance to reach him. The sea just took him and there was no sight of his orange life jacket after one cycle of waves.

The *Yakutat* backed away then. The cutter turned-to and left the *Fort Mercer*. It was well past midnight and there seemed little she could do. The storm was not slackening. The flares from the plane comprised mood lighting for a horror scene, not visibility for a rescue. The survivors would have to hang on until daylight. Further rescues would lead to more harm now. They had to wait for better conditions. Naab felt the worse hour of his life as he realized this, then snapped back to command. There is nothing more we can do now, he thought. We need to just wait until daylight. His own crew had taken a beating in these seas. Everyone was exhausted and they needed some rest. Naab prayed that the old hulk would still be floating.

The four men—Paetzel, Fahrner, Guilden the third mate, and Turner the purser—watched as the rescuers retreated. Where the hell were they going? Guilden found a bell near the forepeak and began ringing it. Paetzel, in the glare of the flares from the plane, took off the flag from his head and waved it wildly skyward.

We're still here, they were saying. We're still alive.

But the plane stopped dropping flares and departed soon after. The *Yakutat* was a good 7 miles away.

Before he turned in, Naab had a thought for what the *Yakutat* might try next. What they needed, Naab thought, was a small boat. And someone like Webber and Bangs. Who did they have? Everyone pointed to Ensign William R. Kiley from Long Branch, New Jersey. He was a big man built like a moose, some said, and he could handle small boats.

What did they have? A Monomoy surfboat, a craft even more ancient than the CG 36500. It had been designed to row through the waves that crashed near Monomoy outside of Chatham, to shoot through such perilous conditions as the Chatham Bar. All the modern technology and this nineteenth-century boat was his best shot, Naab thought.

In the morning, they could see the *Fort Mercer* bow fine. The weather had slacked. Barely, but it had slacked and if nothing else, visibility was better.

What they saw was not encouraging.

The cutter *Yakutat* prepares to launch a motor-powered Monomoy surfboat into 30-foot waves to rescue men on the bow of the *Fort Mercer.*

The *Fort Mercer* bow, already at an angle of forty-five degrees stern to bow, now was at a forty-degree angle to starboard. It was pitching up and over. Water was flooding inside the buoyant tanks that remained. Something had put more stress on the cold steel, something was letting water in and weighting the ship over to the right side—and soon, to capsizing.

Moose Kiley had to be damned good in that boat.

Eleven

THE BAR

February 18, 1952
With Webber—6:00 p.m.

T he wave hung above him and Webber was trying to right the boat before the next big curler crashed down on him. He pulled on the wheel with all his might and gunned the little engine.

But the wave beat him easily and crashed down on the helpless little vessel. It smashed the glass windshield—with the force of a boulder slamming down on a champagne flute—and exploded the glass into Webber's face. Shards missed his eyes but embedded in his skull bone. They stuck out like ornaments. The compass was ripped from its fitting. The canvas canopy was just torn away. Water crashed through the windshield and pulled him away from the wheel—or tried to.

Webber held on with all his might, trying, trying to steer the boat's bow to meet the next wave. The keel, the ton of bronze, was righting them, righting them, bringing them back. He was gunning the engine, powering the boat's bow to the next wave, jamming the throttle, working the gears, while still strapped to the wheel.

Then the third wave crashed onto them and laid them even farther over on their side again in the trough. Worse, the engine failed. The line was gravity feed. The little boat had been so rocked that the gas, like the men, did not know what was up or down. The line had lost its prime and needed to be re-primed. The only way for that to happen was for someone to crawl into the small, enclosed engine room.

Fitzgerald slithered in as the boat was pummeled by the sea. He was thrown against the hot engine block and badly burned, then battered when the boat swung sharply the other way. But he got the engine going, and Webber hit the throttle and they met the next wave head on.

Then the boat did not so much motor as it fell from the top of the next wave into the trough of another, crashing, throwing the men about, the engine shrieking as the props lost grip on the water then grabbed torque and traction, then lost it, falling from the roof of one house-sized peak into the basement-like trough that followed.

The bow was completely airborne one moment, then submerged as the stern tore free of the water. The CG 36500 reeled from one wave, fell, crashed through another, was battered, covered by tons of water, staggered, righted and then roared toward the next breaking wave—like a little halfback throwing off murderous tacklers with no time left on the clock, still heading for the goal.

And then the CG 36500 was through. It had by God crossed the Chatham Bar. But through to what?

The big waves of the deep water came at the boat and still tossed and tore at the vessel, but the CG 36500 could handle these. Some of these monsters, the Coast Guard would later say, were 60 feet in height. Webber strained up the first wave as if he were climbing a mountain. The boat crept slower and slower, like an overloaded roller coaster car, straining, straining.

Then on the other side, he faced a new danger. So steep were the waves, so deep the troughs, that the CG 36500 started speeding faster than ever she had before, gaining great speed and momentum with her 2,000-pound bronze ballast in the keel hauling her downhill very fast.

Now, when they hit the very trough of the wave, the little boat would just keep going—driving her bow, crew, and stern under the water, propelled by the momentum of the one-ton bronze keel.

Webber slammed the engine into reverse in an attempt to slow the boat. Still, she sped down the far side of each wave at an immense speed for the dowdy old girl. Even in reverse, the CG 36500 was speeding down the wave—down the mountain with the bow pointed toward the bottom.

Twelve

AGROUND

February 18, 1952
Aboard the *Pendleton* stern—6:00 p.m.

The *Pendleton* stern drifted parallel to the shore of Cape Cod for a bit, but it was clear that somewhere down the line that parallel path would close with the beach or the rocks. The wind was blowing from shore now. But the waves, the huge waves, and the current carried the half-ship toward the Cape, just as those forces of nature had carried thousands of ships before.

Wallace B. Quirey, the third assistant engineer, dug out his personal shortwave radio. It was not two-way. They could not signal anyone. But it was through the shortwave that they first learned the outside world had learned of them.

They heard the *Fort Mercer* rescue efforts and that cheered them. They knew the Coast Guard was out there. Quirey drank milk and ate eggs. He felt better, stronger.

But then morale sank. They heard nothing about them being in trouble, nothing that gave them hope they had even been sighted. They felt orphaned, abandoned.

And it was around 2 p.m. on Sunday that they sighted land. It was cheering in one sense: there was safety, after all, and firm ground and the promise of warmth and stability.

But the land was also a breaking ground. Worse case scenario? The half-ship would hit rock. Then she could break up very quickly. The men, 1,000 yards from shore perhaps, would be flung into the sea or left to hang onto cold steel without much hope of rescue. Best case scenario? The half-ship would hit soft sand that would keep the ship upright as long as possible.

And so it was that Sybert calculated what he would do. He could steer, some. If he put it full ahead, he could control the direction of the ship a bit. Move it away from the landside and a bit out to sea.

But each time he did that the exposed "bow" of the half-ship bucked and strained and the ship would pitch and yaw. It seemed to be taking on water. The lower engine room seemed to be filling with it. How water-tight would his tanks stay?

It's inevitable, he thought. At some point, we're going to have to go aground. If that was somber news, the men listening to the shortwave soon had an antidote for it. They'd been spotted. They could hear the radio traffic between the cutters and the Navy ship the *Short Splice*. They were talking now not just about the *Fort Mercer*, but about the *Pendleton* as well. They knew a boat had been sent to the *Pendleton* bow. They heard that they had been spotted—that the stern section had been located by the men on land, by radar, and by Coast Guard spotter plane. The plane had flown over at about 4 p.m. and circled them. They had flashed lights at the plane and the plane blinked its lights back at them.

Coast Guard pilot Lt. George Wagner out of Salem, Massachusetts, was above them. He had been working on the *Fort Mercer* stern rescue, and he was relieved and heading home. To his amazement, he saw what he thought to be again the *Fort Mercer* stern. But the colors were all wrong. Was he off course? Fatigued? He radioed in and questions were raised about his navigational competency. He made one low pass and made out the word "Pendleton" on the stern.

So it was yet another tanker, or half-tanker. He followed them then for an hour, radioing to Chatham and other vessels in the area. He watched the *Pendleton* stern drift 6 miles, then move south of Chatham, just a half to three quarters of a mile offshore. He radioed to the *Pendleton* crew, if they could hear him at all.

They were sending a boat. They heard him say that clearly: a boat had been launched from Chatham to rescue them. They could not radio back to the rescuers, but a half-cheer went up in the passageway.

And then Hicks, Steele, and Sybert thought about it. What good was a small boat going to do them? They were 30 feet up in the air above the water. Jumping that distance into a boat? Not likely. And the water temperatures they were taking ranged between thirty-eight and forty-two degrees. This was as close to liquid ice as could be. No one would last long in this water once they were in it. Coast Guard charts would give a man fifteen minutes, if he had a nice built-in wet suit of fat layered about him. Less, ironically, if he were fit and lean.

They needed a ladder or a line of some sort. They had a first-rate ladder for pilots to use, a modern one of steel construction. The pilot would scramble down that ladder once the ship was clear of the harbor. Or he would scramble up it from a pilot boat to bring the ship into harbor.

Where was it stowed? Hicks and Steele were the deck men, the field-promoted officers now. They knew that question all too well. The pilot ladder was on the bow, near the bridge.

Two of the other seamen had an idea though. Down a hatch was an old moldy Jacob's ladder—an old fashioned rope and wood affair from another era of shipping. They used it as a sort of draft marker. They'd throw it over the side to see what sort of water the ship was drawing for an informal measurement of the bottom.

Hicks and Steele looked at the contraption. The top rope seemed rotten and a few steps were missing. On the bottom? The next-to-last rung was gone. But it was better than nothing and they spread it out along the deck.

Hicks and Sybert were taking drafts now not with the Jacob's ladder but with a leaded line that gave them more precise readings. They were okay for now. But inevitably they were closing at an acute angle with the shore.

Sybert decided it then: the boat was on the way. He could hear the boatman—it must have been Bernie—say he was forty-five minutes out, maybe. It looked as if there was a smooth sandbar not far away. He asked how the waves were breaking on the bar, and Quirey answered they were breaking smooth on the bar. It was daylight still. Lord knows what lay ahead in the night: blind uncertainty and the chance of rocks. They were maneuvering and the ship was lurching even more now, listing forty degrees to port.

"Stop!" Sybert said. "We had better go on the beach than capsize."

And so he put the ship aground then: stopped the maneuvering of the engines and let the ship drift in on the bar. She touched the sand sweetly with only a bit of rock and sway.

The men hunkered down in the passageway. Sybert told the engineers to secure the engine room and come topside. He did not want them trapped a dozen feet below if the compartments gave way. Already, the lower engine room was deep in water.

He thought about launching the lifeboats then. Perhaps that was the way to go: lower the men in the lifeboats and head for shore. He looked down the rail at the waves. They were churning, foaming monsters. Some were 20 feet, some were 45 feet; they came at sequences of 30 to 40 feet. A lifeboat would have little chance in such water. It would swamp almost immediately, even if it could be launched.

So the two-man watches were maintained and the men in the passageway kept their spirits up and ignored as best they could the fact that the ship was leaning and listing ever more sideward. She was turned sideward to the sea now on a sandbar and the waves battered in below.

Whatever ballistics in the water she may have had were gone now and she sat stranded on the bar, a stub of a ship in the surf, taking a pounding.

It was about 7 p.m. and dark when one of the lookouts thought he saw something moving out there: a light, a little light. It grew larger and from out of the 45-foot waves he saw an audacious little lifeboat, searchlight probing here and there.

"There's a boat alongside the starboard side!" he yelled back to the men.

There was a tendency to surge forward now.

"Take it easy," Sybert said. "Calm yourselves."

Then he left the passageway. He peered down at the cork of a boat bobbing below, then went back for the men.

Line up on the starboard side, he said, and they fanned out into the wind. Hicks and Steele grabbed the Jacob's ladder and began to tie it to the rail. They could feel the ship list even farther to port. The ship would rock out and in, rock out and in.

Steele looked down at the CG 36500 and wondered, How in God's name did these guys do this?

Thirteen

WATERFALLS

February 18, 1952
With Webber—evening

Webber's little boat was heading straight down the wave and toward the bottom of the ocean when finally the propellers, thrown hard into reverse, caught and helped slow the boat. At the bottom of the wave, in the valley of the watery mountain, the bow broke through the water and was buried. But buoyancy brought the boat back up quickly. Webber slammed the gear into forward and the CG 36500 now began to crawl slowly *up* the new mountain of a wave in front of her.

So now what? Webber thought. They had survived the bar and were cruising up and down the huge storm rollers. But their compass was gone. They were in pitch darkness and blizzard white-out simultaneously. Radio contact was spotty at best. Webber just pointed the boat where he thought the *Pollock Rip* lightship *might* be. He could get directions from there.

They were all shivering, all very cold and wet. Webber lost track of time. In the darkness, he peered out through his shattered windshield. At times, he saw lights out there, and then realized light was playing off the shards of glass stuck near his eyes, still embedded there in bone. He tried to pluck them out. Some came loose. Others broke off. Still others could not be budged.

His plan was to head for the *Pollock Rip* lightship, but he was having no luck finding it. He radioed in but there was no reply. After a time, he saw a shadow that was darker than the darkness. It creeped him out at first; it was spooky and made him uncomfortable. He slowed the boat, nearly to a stop. Turn on the spotlight, Webber told a crew member. Someone scrambled out on the bow and switched the light on, but a wave caught the bow of the boat and the crew member was tossed in the air, just gone.

Then a second later, there was a large thump in the boat. When Webber looked, the crew member was back, claimed by the sea but then spat back on the boat. Webber had no time to check on the man's condition. He was in a world of spook and wonder, danger too for that matter. He motored slowly forward and saw what he took to be the entrance to a tunnel, a tunnel they were headed into. Broken and twisted steel and wires marked the entrance to this tunnel and it rose up in the water with each wave and then settled back, exhaling masses of foam. Each time it rose, waterfalls cascaded from it. Each time it fell, Webber thought, the clang of loose steel sounded as if the "tunnel" were groaning in pain. It had to be the *Pendleton*.

Warily, Bernie maneuvered the CG 36500. He moved along the port side of the hulk. There were no signs of life. Up above, steel railings were bent like pipe cleaners. All this way they had come, and no one was left alive, Webber thought. His heart sank at the uselessness of their effort.

He turned the spotlight on the stern and confirmed what they had found. The word "Pendleton" was painted on the ship's hull. Then he rounded the hull and saw what looked like lights up there on the starboard side of the deck. Webber saw the lights, then one man. He looked as tiny as an ant. Webber said to himself, *Holy shit! The four of us came all this way for one man.*

Then the man left the rail, but why? Webber soon found out. Dozens of men crowded to the railing and yelled down to Webber, cheering.

Webber looked up at the scene in absolute and utter awe. Men ringed the rail of the ship and sent up a weak cheer. The cheer swept over the Coast Guardsmen like warm rain. It made their spines tingle and they all felt a surge of pride and adrenaline. Webber thought for a moment on how this all would work now. Now that they were here, how would they take them down? His answer came in the form of the Jacob's ladder fluttering and banging down the side of the hull as the ship pitched.

Bernie brought the boat in closer to the ladder. He peered up at the ship and could not help but think it. Guys, we should go *up* the ladder and wait for help. That half-ship seemed a lot sturdier than did the CG 36500.

But he said nothing. He did not have time to. Already, men were clambering down the ladder. The tanker men were coming home.

Fourteen

DOWNWARD BOUND

February 18, 1952
The *Pendleton* stern and the CG 36500—8:00 p.m.

S teele and Hicks and James Young, the chief pumpman, tossed the Jacob's ladder over the side. It twisted and fouled and they had to hoist it back up. The second time, the ladder accordioned out down the side of the ship's hull and dangled into the waves below.

Normally, the departure would be in terms of seniority, with the lowest rank going first and the officers staying behind. But this was a perilous venture—not an easy trip down a flight of stairs, but an unknown descent into fierce seas.

So Steele, it was decided, would go first. The able-bodied seaman was just that—as fit as anyone there. He would chart the way down.

Over he went. He did not like the top of the ladder. It seemed rotten both in rope and wood. But he did not tarry at the top. Down he went, with 4- to 5-foot gaps between the wooden plank steps. You had to have some upper body strength to do this. Hold on as you reached down with your foot almost an entire body length to the next plank. Slide down a bit with your hands, feet dangling for purchase on the next rung.

And the rock and the roll of the ship and the sea made it like no trip off a ship Steele had ever experienced. The ship listed to port so at times the ladder was close in to the starboard side of the hull. Then the ship would rock and he would swing out then slam back into the hull.

The waves were a force that changed like swirling clouds. One moment, Steele would look up and 20 feet above his head, he would see a wave curling like a house of liquid. Then it would drop with a *woomph* as the cycle moved past and he would look down into a valley, a hole really, that was now 20 feet *below* his head.

There was no fixed point if he looked out there. And there was nothing much he could do but keep going down. The last step was a tough one: two lengths down, for a plank was missing.

But when he got to the bottom rung, there was the CG 36500. Webber had timed it perfectly. He had made his pass just as Steele hit the bottom, and the seamen, taken by the arms by the crew, stepped gingerly aboard the small boat.

Once onboard, Steele saw how bad it was. These were not so much "passes" that Webber was making at the ship. It was more like a bumper-car. The wooden boat would slam into the hull, bounce off, and Webber would bring it around again.

Harnessed still to the wheel, the young coxswain needed three hands to run the CG 36500: one for the wheel, one for the throttle and speed, one for the direction and gear shift of the boat. He was in constant motion and the shifting, the turning, none of it was on automatic power. Each shift, turn, and gear change took real physical effort.

"Where are your fenders?" Steele yelled to the crewmen. Where are the padded protectors that boats carried to protect against damage when moored at dockside? Below, one of the crew members said, and Steele scurried down, found them, fetched them topside, and rigged a few in place, hoping they would protect the CG 36500.

Above him, the rope was crowded with men descending. Hicks, still on deck, had seen Steele make his passage and decided that the older and weaker should go first now. They stood a better chance the sooner they were off and the fewer people were on the boat.

So down they came. And Webber, looking up, thought to himself, *My God, how many of them are there?* The CG 36500 was rated to carry twenty. There were a hell of a lot more than twenty. He would have to make two trips.

And he knew the futility of that thought. Even if he and his men and his boat could physically make the run, the *Pendleton* stern would not last. It was listing ever more precariously. Bernie had no desire to climb upon this hulk now. She was about to go over.

He made a decision then, a resolution and vow to himself. Either we all make it out, or none of us do. If there are fifty men up there, we try for all fifty. No one gets left behind.

The men continued down the ladder. Some of them timed the boat just right. Above them, engineer Edward Gallagher and others would wait for the right synch of wave, boat, and man on the ladder and yell, "Jump!" Most times, this worked.

When it didn't, Bernie's crew was right there. If someone missed the boat, well, Livesey, Fitzgerald, and Maske were right there. They were filled with adrenaline. They would reach down, singly and together, and grab a man by his jacket, his arms, his belt, and give a mighty hoist.

Most were sent below. They needed to pack in passengers carefully now if they were to have any chance of handling everyone. The system was working methodically. Bernie would maneuver, be hurled toward the ship, back off in reverse, gun the engines, swerve in, swing the wheel, heave-to under the ladder—and the men jumped. The ladder swerved and banged and skipped about. It dunked them up and down in the ocean as if they were teabags. But they all came down. For those who hit the water, it was tuna fishing time. They were hurled on board, then sent below.

Six men were left on top when Aaron Ponsel and Tiny Myers were next down the ladder. All night, they had been blowing the whistle. Now it was time to leave.

Ponsel scampered down easily and ran to the stern of the ship, ready to go below. He turned to see Tiny cumbersomely ease down the ladder. He was very heavy and very tired, with little strength left. The 4 to 5 feet in between rungs were a struggle for him. Waves slammed against him and it seemed as if he had lost his pants up there. The ladder would bow out with the sway of the half-ship, and then slam Tiny hard back against the steel hull. Webber thought he could hear the big man groan. It was a bizarre scene, this huge man, nearly naked, struggling down the ladder.

And then Myers came to the bottom rung of the ladder, the last rung. The one that was a double length away from the next one up because a rung was missing. Strength seemed to go out of the big man then, and he hit the last rung with his feet and then with his knees. He was kneeling on the last rung, but it all looked lined up. The boat was there. "Jump!" someone yelled. It was unclear whether Tiny jumped or slipped.

The boat was there. And then it was not. Wave action pulled it away and Tiny hit a part of the boat, then went into the water. Immediately, hands were on him. Not just the CG 36500 crew but the hands of the crew of the *Pendleton* as well. They had him. They could get him.

But they could not get him into the boat. He could not lift his leg up over the gunnels; he had no strength or energy left. And when they reached down to grab him, they could get no good purchase. His pants and belt, a normal grasping point, were gone. His jacket let them lift him up, but not over. Watersoaked as he was, the men were attempting to dead lift four hundred pounds or so.

So they held him there. All the time, other men were coming down. Some hit the boat. Some missed it. Bernie needed to maneuver to reach them. They were coming whether he wanted them to or not.

Young, the pumpman, was one of the men grabbing Tiny when a wave picked up the boat and jammed it toward the hull.

"Watch out, you are going to hit your head on the ship!" Steele yelled out. Young kept hold of Tiny Myers, and Steele grabbed Young and pulled him back. Tiny slipped down as the boat rammed against the hull, and against Tiny. Richard Livesey, the CG 36500 crew member, still had a hand on Tiny and his hand was crushed between the boat and the hull. He let go.

The crew caught Tiny with their spotlight. They could still see him. He was floating. They were perilously close to the ship's hull. Men were still coming down and landing on the boat, landing in the water. Tiny drifted toward the propeller of the ship. Webber could see him; he was still alive and their eyes locked. It was a look from Tiny, Webber thought, that said, "It's okay. It's okay."

There was only one way to get to Tiny, Webber thought, and that was to ease the bow to him and have the crew grab him. Myers was in a narrow area of the ship near the prop, and the CG 36500 could not approach him broadside.

So he turned the bow toward Tiny, eyes on his eyes the entire time. And then the sea caught the CG 36500 and pushed her forward against Myers's chest and crushed the big man against the stern of the *Fort Mercer*.

The impact on the crew was devastating. But they could not tarry. There were still men coming down, still live men in the water. The crew turned the searchlight away from Tiny Myers and toward the living.

David A. Brown, the first assistant engineer, was the last man down the ladder. He made a smooth descent. Sybert was already on board; along with Bernie and the others, they directed the men here and there, packing them into whatever spaces were available.

Webber confirmed there were no more men on board. He made a head count and confirmed it with Sybert. They had thirty-two men out of thirty-three onboard.

Webber keyed the mike on his radio and made history with those simple words. This is the CG 36500, he said in effect, and we have thirty-two of thirty-three survivors from the stern of the *Pendleton*. We are heading home.

Behind them, before they left, just twenty minutes after the last man was down, the stern of the *Pendleton* took another list, creaked and groaned as tanks collapsed.

Then it capsized and rolled sidewards into the sea, its decks awash.

The stern of the *Pendleton* shortly after it rolled over just twenty minutes after the last crewman was evacuated.

Fifteen

MORNING

February 19, 1952
Aboard the bow of the *Fort Mercer*—8:30 a.m.

The four men on the bow of the *Fort Mercer* had huddled together all night—with Guilden ringing the bell, with the captain, when he thought he saw a ship's light or a plane, waving the flag he held on his head like a scarf.

Then, as dawn came, they saw the lights of the *Yakutat* grow ever-closer. From the leaden clouds of morning at the edge of the sea, the profile of the cutter formed and then filled in form as it came closer.

Soon the ship was in hailing distance, and a *Yakutat* officer explained the new deal. It was clearer now—not much calmer, but clearer—and they could see. Rather than the men jumping to them, the *Yakutat* would send a boat. The men would line up on the rail and one-by-one jump for the boat.

On the half-ship, the officers and the purser huddled. Paetzel was near gone. Still in his bare feet, he stomped about on his frostbitten feet, just hanging in there. Tradition and rank had it that the cap was the last man to leave the ship. Paetzel insisted on it. Common sense told

Fahrner and Guilden that they were stronger and that the captain and the purser should be the first.

So they told him then and there: you go first. Paetzel said no. Then we'll throw you over first, the two junior officers told him. Your choice.

And so that is how Paetzel went first. They edged down the deck toward midships of the half-ship. It was perilous. It was a Tilt-A-Whirl ride in the seas now. The ship pointed up at its same forty-five-degree angle, but now the list to starboard was around forty-five to fifty degrees. Something below was giving way. The waterproof tanks were crumpling. Buoyancy was being lost as air pockets seeped out and turned the ship ever more perilously toward capsizing.

The officers looked out from the bow of the *Fort Mercer* and what they saw was a very large man in a very small boat. The *Yakutat* had lowered a Monomoy surfboat with Kiley and his crew into waves that still crested at 30 to 45 feet. The seas had not calmed at all, just the snow and the rain. They dropped the surfboat on davits into the drink and instantly, Kiley was on the ride of his life. The boat was well built but less than 30 feet long—far shorter than Bernie's CG 36500 and without deck covering.

Just keeping the craft moving forward was a challenge. Where was forward? The waves lifted the small craft up like a cork—one story, two stories, three stories, four stories above the "ground floor"—then dropped it into a basement four stories below that. The seas would make the small boat run before them, then spin the craft about while the wind tugged it in another direction.

Riley had only a tiller steer on the boat and no wheel. The difference between Riley and the lifesaver of a century ago was a power engine. That was about it.

Still he made it. Moose Kiley crossed the gap between the *Yakutat* and the *Fort Mercer* bow and at first approached the starboard side, the lower side. But that was also where the heaviest seas were breaking and he saw this was no good.

Off to portside then, and he was there in front of them now, the officers lined by the railing.

Jump, he mouthed to Paetzel, as the lifeboat made a pass, and Paetzel leaped from the railing. He struck frozen feet first into the water, as he had intended. His life jacket popped him to the surface and all seemed well. Then the sea sucked him into the eddy of the half-hull of the ship. The sea hammered him there, then spat him back away from the ship.

Kiley's crew had him, for a moment. One of the crew members had a boathook and he thrust it out to Paetzel and the captain grabbed it for all he was worth. Then the sea corkscrewed them about again and the leverage of it all twisted the boathook handle and all away from the crewman. Paetzel bobbed numbly in the water, holding on tightly to the boathook and handle, which no one held on the other side.

After a while, he let the boathook float loose, as he lost it and drifted—ever more numb now—toward unconsciousness. A line came hurtling through the air across him from the boat. He missed it. A second line was thrown out then. And again, Paetzel missed it. He did not know where he was now. A third line flew from the boat and Paetzel never remembered grabbing it. But he did. And they had him. They hauled him to the side of the boat and heaved him over. Paetzel flopped into the boat and was safe.

At the same time, seas flowed over the dipped down the side of the boat and drenched the rescuers. Water filled much of the bottom of the little craft now and it wallowed more in the big waves. Somewhere there, too, as Kiley fought to find the captain and bring him aboard, the little boat had slammed hard against the hull of the half-ship and no one was quite sure whether the wooden sides were stove in or not.

Still, they rounded about toward the *Fort Mercer* bow. Turner, the purser, was next. He jumped. He caught a line. He was in. Over the side he came as they leveraged him in from the sea. And over the side again came a tub or two of water, near swamping the little boat.

Kiley wallowed about in the seas with his damaged boat, half-swamped and half-afloat. He looked up at Guilden and Fahrner, the third and second mates, and he did not have to tell them; they knew. He had to go, and go now.

He rounded the little boat past the bow of the *Fort Mercer* and waved to the officers on board, then rounded to again and headed back to the *Yakutat.*

Guilden and Fahrner watched them go. Fahrner had never seen seamanship like that. He had watched in amazement as Kiley brought the little boat in—up and over the huge waves, swirls, and eddies; timing it just right to get as close as he could to the boat and the men.

Now they watched Kiley head back to the cutter. It was more than a mile to the *Yakutat.* They would catch sight of the little boat, then watch it completely disappear down a wave. Then bob to the top of the crest of another wave, and slide down and disappear down the side of another.

They both knew there was as much a chance the boat would not make it. Perhaps it would be back for them—but more likely it would not make it back.

They could not see the mile to the *Yakutat* as Kiley brought the surf-boat home. He was wallowing awfully now, just making headway, the boat half-sunk as he pulled to the leeward side of the *Yakutat.*

They had thought to bring the boat up on davits, but it was nearly sinking at shipside, so they brought the men up by cargo nets. Then, the little boat was lifted up as well. All the time, Kiley protested. He could make another run, he told Naab. He could do it again. One more time, Kiley said. He was sobbing now. Naab and the others thought it a miracle Kiley had even made it back at all. They would not let him go out again.

Paetzel and Turner were rushed to warm blankets and beds. They were beat and battered. They were in better shape than the little Monomoy, though. The boat would not go out again this day.

And the cutter, an hour later, approached the half-ship again and hailed Guilden and Fahrner and told them that. The officers could hear the Coast Guardsman over the loudspeaker, or at least they could hear enough. The wind, the waves, the howl of it all carried away some of the words. But they got the drift of what was happening now in bits and spurts, some clear, some blown away by the wind.

We're going to shoot you a line … tie it fast to the rail … we'll run you a raft … jump to the raft.… Noise drowned out the words then, but they got the gist. Jump to the raft and the Coast Guard would pull them in. And so they set about it.

The Coast Guard fired a line. This time, on the first try it arched over the bow of the *Fort Mercer* and the men caught it. They hauled on the thin line and brought on board a heavier line.

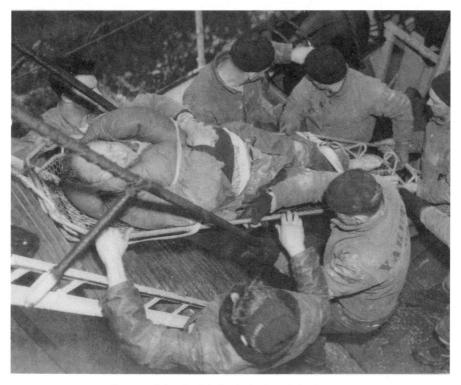

Rescuers bring Captain Paetzel onboard the *Yakutat*.

Across the pitching ocean, they could see the Coast Guardsmen dump a raft into the sea. The raft had one line tied to the cutter and the Coasties were paying out that line. The two men on the *Fort Mercer* bow hauled on the line and the raft edged ever closer to the bow. The men ached with cold, but they could haul and haul they did.

Soon the raft was about 30 yards away. They judged that about right. Any closer and it might be pushed into the bow. Any farther? They had no chance.

And now seniority kicked in. Guilden, who had lined himself to Fahrner earlier, was the third mate. And Fahrner, the second, would be the last man off.

They wished each other luck and then Guilden was on the line to the raft, on the far side of the *Fort Mercer* rail, and then he was gone. Fahrner was alone on the rail now.

Guilden slid as far as he could on the line, about half way to the raft, then plunged into the sea. Crushing cold! The sea took his breath away, but he swam, struck out across the 10 to 15 yards to the raft and he was there.

But there was one problem. The life raft had flipped and it was upside down to the water. Men have died in cold waters clinging to the sides of life rafts properly righted. That last foot or so of vertical barrier might just as well be a 100-foot cliff, so drained are the men and so numb; they can summon no strength to gain purchase on the sheer rubber and canvas raft sides.

Guilden for a moment simply held onto the raft. Then he fought the cold and the fatigue. For more than fourteen hours, he and those on the bow had been stressed beyond endurance and they had endured. Now he tried everything he could. Sheer strength lifting the raft would not work. It simply leveraged him below the water.

But he still had his wits and after a bit thought he saw how to work it. From the railing, Fahrner watched as his third mate maneuvered the edge of the raft in the seas and the wind; the convergence of the seas and the wind managed to lift a corner of the raft up, then lifted it up more and lofted it skyward for a moment, then flopped it over, upright.

From the bridge of the *Yakutat*, Commander Naab watched and thought Guilden's struggle superhuman. How could he do something like that? How could he survive in those waters period, yet right the raft?

Guilden was quite human, though. Having righted the raft, he could only hold on. He was wholly spent. He simply drifted next to the raft, a limp arm wrapped atop the side. He was unable to hoist himself over the top and looked as if he might drift off at any moment.

Fahrner on the rail knew he had to act fast. Yes, he wanted to help Guilden, who had so valiantly lashed himself to Fahrner when Fahrner had no life vest. But he needed to act fast for another reason. He could feel the bow shifting. The starboard list had moved to sixty degrees now. The half-ship was capsizing and about to roll.

The little Monomoy surfboat makes its way back through huge waves to the *Yakutat* with mariners rescued from the *Fort Mercer* bow.

Still, he calculated what to do. He planned it. He saw how Guilden had slipped off the rope. Fahrner untied the rope from the rail and slacked off more length into the water. Better to enter the water and pull himself along the rope than attempt to slide in the air, drop off, and swim without the rope.

From the *Yakutat*, the Coasties watched earnestly. This was all going according to plan, or as much as it could. They had told the men what to do. Slide down to the raft and then the last man would undo the rope from the rail of the sinking bow and swim for the raft. Then the Coast Guard would pull them in.

And that was what Fahrner was doing. He had undone the rope and … then he was retying the rope! What was happening? He was lashing the raft line to the bow again. Not the plan. *Not* the plan.

What had happened is that the wind and waves had carried those last instructions away. The ship officers simply had not heard them.

Neither were they green nor dumb. Their plan was to simply cut the rope when they got to the raft. Guilden carried a large sheath knife on his belt. Fahrner had a large clasp knife safely in his pocket. If you were on board a ship, you almost always carried a knife. You never knew when you might have to cut a line.

So Fahrner never thought twice about the raft remaining tethered. He jumped for it and hit the water well. He felt the same breath-sucking cold then struck out for the raft. He reached it, grabbed, then got entangled in his own lines. He struggled for a moment before freeing himself.

Then he came up alongside Guilden and gave him words of encouragement. And he was smart enough to know what to do. It was akin to the instructions air attendants would give countless fliers in more modern times. In event of depressurization, parents should put on their oxygen masks first, then help their children.

And Fahrner, while he still had strength, lifted himself into the raft rather than try to push Guilden up. In the raft, Fahrner could have leverage and more strength. In the water, he would soon tire with no leverage. In attempting to push Guilden up, he would simply push himself down. And then both men would be cold and clinging to the raft: dead men floating.

Still, once in the raft, it was no easy trick. The raft's wall was a slick cliff. Guilden could not scale it; Fahrner could not dead-lift his comrade and his water-soaked clothes. It took five minutes of struggle for the men to time the waves and the water just right, and then Guilden was half over the side of the raft, and then into it.

Both men lay in the bottom of the raft, cold and exhausted. But they had made it. Now they needed only to cut the raft loose and the Coasties would haul them in. Guilden reached for the knife in his sheath on his belt. It was gone. The sea had twisted it loose. Fahrner was happy he had his clasp knife firmly in his pocket. And he reached for it now. They would cut the line and be gone.

Such a simple thing. Just open a pocket knife, a large pocket knife. Fahrner had the knife in his hands. He was commanding his fingers to grasp the blade, hold it against his thumb and just apply the half pound of pressure needed to open the blade.

His fingers did not respond. He could not feel them. He could not make them move. They might as well be stumpy pegs of half-frozen meat. In fact, they were. Untie the knot then? A worse idea. If he could not open the knife, how could he untie a taught knot drawn tighter by the pounding of the seas?

Fahrner looked across at the *Yakutat*, then back at the bow of the *Fort Mercer*. The bow was tilting ever more starboard now, about to roll. The bow was going to take them with her: they were lashed to her and they had no way to break the tie.

On the bridge of the *Yakutat*, Commander Naab, the architect of the diverse *Fort Mercer* bow rescue attempts, was now at a loss. The poor bastards in the raft were caught between the devil of the deep blue sea and the angel of mercy, his very own *Yakutat*. But what could he do now? The two lines held the men in mid-ocean. The bow was sinking even now as they looked at her. What could he do?

Only one thing. Pull the wishbone and hope he got the right piece. He would have to back off the cutter, power it away from the sinking hulk and hope and pray that the right line broke.

If the line from raft to tanker broke, their wish came true and they got the big half of the wishbone and the men in the raft. If the line from the *cutter* to the raft broke, the men would still be tethered to the bow. And anyone could see that the bow was going any minute, any second. It would sink and drag the men to their dead friends.

Wilfred Bleakley, a young ensign on the bridge of the *Yakutat* just eight months out of the Coast Guard Academy, could stand it no longer. "You have no choice, Captain!" he bleated out. "Back down and hope the line breaks on the other side of the raft." Pull the wishbone and pray you got the big piece with the raft on it.

Officers from the bow of the *Fort Mercer* huddle in a life raft.

Naab pretty much had that figured out without the ensign's advice. Then again, he had to admit it, the kid was right. Back down, Naab ordered.

The big cutter backed down, began moving away. The lines on both sides became taught, stretching, throwing off water and straining.

Then there was a snap, a crack as if a large caliber rifle had been fired.

Sixteen

MORE ORDERS

February 18, 1952
With Webber—late evening

T here was exuberance and disbelief in the Chatham Coast Guard station when Webber's radio message came through. Impossible! They
had figured Webber for dead.

But the glee was quickly replaced by rapid fire questions, both from
the Coast Guard station and the Coast Guard cutters attending to the
Fort Mercer. Send him out to sea and we will take the passengers off on
a cutter, one officer said. Another disagreed, and there was an argument
over jurisdiction, over rank, over anything.

Webber, twenty-four years old, was shivering and near exhaustion.
These guys weren't helping. He did not have to think about it this time.
There is a time to follow the book and a time to throw it away.

They were going to guide him in? They didn't know where *he* was; he
didn't know where *they* were. How was that supposed to work? One of
the officers on the big cutters directed him to come alongside the cutter
and transfer the seamen to the cutter. How was *that* going to work? He
had just done the near-impossible getting these men *down* a ladder and

off a ship. Many of them had fallen. How was he going to get them *up* a ladder in these waters? He did not think they would fall up.

They weren't here. He was. Bernie Webber, so easily led in his youth, was leading now. He reached to the radio and then simply flipped it off.

He knew where *he* was going. He was going home to Chatham. He was heading home to Miriam. But most of all he knew he was responsible for thirty-two souls saved from the sea. That's how he thought of it. He had thirty-two souls at sea to save and no one else could make the right calls now. He raised his voice above the wind and said something close to this: "Fellas, here's what we're going to do. We got out here heading into the sea and we will get out of here with the seas on our butt. We will hit land sometime somewhere that way. If we have to beach, get ready to get out quickly."

The word was passed along throughout the boat to those who did not hear it. And from the packed mass of *Pendleton* crew members, someone said, "We're with you Coxswain!" And then spontaneously a cheer arose from the rescued seamen.

They motored on for an hour. The engine would die at times; the gravity feed was too jostled to get gas to the engine and Fitzgerald would crawl in, burn himself, and prime the pump. They would sputter and motor on in silence. Bernie figured the worst that could happen is they would hit land and a beach somewhere and he'd just run it aground. Or they would drift into Nantucket Channel and relative shelter, then know where they were.

Webber had no idea where he was. In deep water, the waves were steep but spaced far apart, with wide valleys in between the mountains of water. So he knew he was still at sea. The boat itself was silent. Men were packed everywhere. They shivered. They clung to the boat. But they did not talk. There was the low roar of the motor, the screech still of the wind, and the crash and slap of waves as they crested over the covered deck. Time passed and the scene was unchanged. Webber wondered what he had done and what he was doing. Had he made the right decisions?

Then he noticed that the waters had changed. The big waves and broad valleys of the ocean became rougher and the cycles shorter. The waves were not quite as big as the at-sea soaring rollers nor as rhythmic or patterned. The seas became "confused" in the parlance of mariners and Bernie knew he was now heading into shallower water. They pitched and yawed and it seemed to a few of the men onboard that they touched bottom at least twice. Definitely, they were in the shallows now. Livesey and some seamen were packed together like sardines at the back of the boat and water kept washing over them, sometimes over their heads. Livesey was having trouble breathing. He hoped Bernie knew where he was.

He didn't. Webber knew only that they had reached shallower water. But where? Bernie thought perhaps North Beach, an isolated area where they could find little shelter from this cold and little refuge for his cargo of frozen souls.

Then Bernie began hallucinating again, or he thought he was. He thought he saw a red light. But he had thought he had seen lights before only to find out the shards of glass in his head were playing tricks of reflection on him.

Now this time? It was a flashing red light. Truly he was seeing things. For the light would be high above him at one moment. He'd look again and it was below him in the sea. It was in the sky, then it was in the sea. It's the glass, the snow, the salt spray, all playing tricks on me, he concluded. I've got to stay calm here.

But the red light persisted and Bernie knew what it had to be. There was an aircraft warning light on the Chatham RCA radio station tower. To be that high up in the sky, it had to be the RCA tower. The bad news was they seemed headed toward North Beach and isolation. What was the next step there? How could he give them shelter there?

Well, it was *something* and Bernie steered toward the light. Up in the air he could see it one moment, then far below another. This was perplexing. The light was not behaving like a tower beacon at all. They seemed to be approaching the light in the water and when they got a bit closer, Bernie told his crew to shine a searchlight toward the light.

There was utter surprise, then elation. The searchlight caught a buoy. The light was on a buoy, and Bernie had enough time in these waters to know which buoy. It was the buoy on the *inside* of the Chatham Bar. That choppy water they crossed *was* the bar. The light in the sky and then down below was the buoy bobbing up with the monstrous waves then down into the valley of the waves.

Now they were in safe waters—or at least safer waters. They had somehow found their way back through the storm and retraced their rough course out. Now all Bernie had to do was navigate the twists and turns of the channel and he was home-free.

Once in this smoother water beyond the bar and inside the harbor, Bernie Webber keyed his radio and said: "This is CG 36500. We're inside the harbor heading to the Chatham Fish Pier."

There was shock and disbelief that the CG 36500 had reached the harbor. It lasted about two seconds before Webber again got a series of confusing instructions on the radio. He was to turn this way, then that way. Webber instinctively followed the first few commands, and then realized someone was trying to guide him in with the experimental radar. Everyone wanted to show that the expensive new equipment was of some help.

Webber did not try to be polite. He called the watchtower and said essentially that the only help he needed was when they got back to the fish pier. Perhaps someone could be there to help the survivors. Then he snapped the radio off again. He knew these waters. He was here; they weren't.

Steadily through the harbor, the CG 36500 parted through the calmer waves. The crew and the survivors could all see the lights of the Chatham Fish Pier. Now, the little boat came to life. Some of the survivors were thanking God aloud. Others were sobbing. Many more were talking with each other rapidly. Many of them were crammed together down below, knowing only that they were in calmer waters.

Bernie looked up at the pier as they motored in.

From a distance, it looked like the whole town was there.

For the first time in more than twelve hours, Webber felt warmth. It flooded over him. Warmth and a strange comfort.

Seventeen

THE WISHBONE

February 19, 1952
Aboard the *Yakutat*—10:30 a.m.

There was a snap as if a rifle had been fired, and Naab and the others aboard the *Yakutat* peered out to see how the wishbone had split.

The raft jerked suddenly and jolted toward the cutter. The line to the bow of the *Fort Mercer* snapped in two, shot toward the bow, and then slacked in the water.

Immediately, the Coast Guard hauled on the other line. They heaved and in about ten minutes they had the raft alongside the *Yakutat*. Guilden and Fahrner were exhausted, stretched out in the boat.

At that exact moment, someone yelled, "There she goes!"

The survivors, still in the raft, looked over at the bow section. The half-ship turned over and sank the bow deck beneath the waves. Then the survivors swiveled their frozen necks and looked up at the Coast Guard. Ensign Bleakley would never forget the look on their faces—a combination of wonder, gratefulness, exhaustion, and amazement.

Coast Guard rescuers prepare to bring the last two survivors from the bow of the *Fort Mercer* onboard the *Yakutat*.

Eighteen

HOME

February 18, 1952
Chatham—11:30 p.m.

Photographer Dick Kelsey was local to Cape Cod. He watched the big city newspaper boys carefully as they jockeyed for position. All of them were lined up at the Chatham Fish Pier as if it were the 50-yard line of the Rose Bowl. Like Kelsey, they held in their hands the big, cumbersome Speed Graphic cameras of the day, the type that used huge #2 flash bulbs and film holders.

Kelsey plotted out how he would play this. He planned his shots. All of them would have a shot of the little lifeboat as it came in. And then they would walk from the cold and into the warmth of the Coast Guard lifeboat station. He thought about that. They were heading to the kitchen area of the Coast Guard station and he'd been there before. Just about everything there threw off humidity: the radiators, the coffee urns, the wet clothes drying on radiators. It was like a steam bath up there. Kelsey knew what he was going to do. If he was right, this was going to give him an edge.

In Chatham Harbor, the traditional town village meeting had been underway when someone came running in. Quickly, the townspeople surged to the pier in Old Harbor. Snow was still falling, and there was that snow globe feeling.

And from out of the dark, the lights of CG 36500 shown dimly at first, then grew brighter and larger, and then showed the boat itself. A cheer went up from the wharf as Webber steered the boat to dockside.

One-by-one, in what seemed an endless parade, the merchant seamen emerged from the small boat. The villagers cheered them on and the sailors faintly cheered back. In tone, it was a scene from an old black-and-white movie from the 1930s. The passengers just seemed to keep emerging from impossible spaces, somewhat like one of those college stunts where students attempt to pack people in a car.

A barrage of flash bulbs fired from the wharf as the press photographers triggered their Speed Graphics. Flash and fire. Then they would

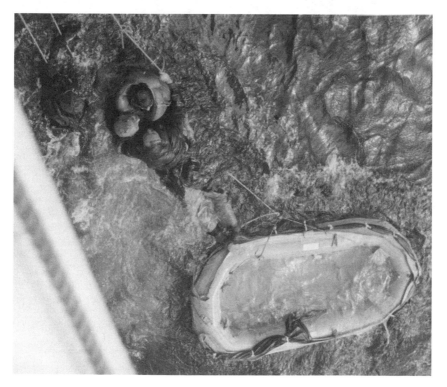

The men from the raft are hoisted aboard the *Yakutat*.

The survivors of the *Fort Mercer* bow. Captain Paetzel is in the bunk.

reload with new bulbs and a new photographic frame. The action of the men and the boat were caught in discolike strobes. Kelsey was in there too. He got some good shots. The men were heading toward the warmth of the Coast Guard station and the pack of press photographers were headed that way, too. All of them packed into cars and trucks and drove the mile from the Fish Pier to the lifeboat station.

Kelsey wasn't worried. He lagged behind on purpose and watched as just Bernie and one other crewman were on board. Webber stood there for a long moment just braced against the wheel, resting. Kelsey took the shot. Then he carefully unscrewed his frozen lens from the camera front, placed it inside his coat, and held it tight against his armpit. He patted the lens inside his coat and then slowly drove to the Coast Guard station.

Onboard the boat, the boat crew filed out and followed the mariners. "Thanks Webb," Livesey said softly, as if they had just done a supply run to the lighthouse.

Webber and Maske were alone on the boat when Bernie released it all. He began sobbing and convulsed with tears—exhausted, cold, in grief for the lost man. The twenty-four-year-old cried openly with wracking sobs that shook his whole body. He just shook for a long while, then looked out to sea, then at the men a distance away, alive on land. Then he took a breath and headed toward the Coast Guard station.

There, the big city press boys were cursing and swearing and wiping madly at their lenses. It did no good. The warm air on the cold lenses produced fog. Kelsey brought out his warmed lens, patiently screwed it back onto his Speed Graphic and began snapping the bizarre scenes in front of him. The warmed lens did not fog and Kelsey allowed himself a bit of wry chuckle at this triumph of tradecraft. The Associated Press would use his pictures on the wire that week. They went worldwide.

Nearly the whole town, it seemed, had turned out. Roy Anderson of the Red Cross was handing out blankets. There was Benny Shufro of Puritan Clothing, measuring a seaman for a new pair of pants. Others were ladling out soup while others were pouring cups of coffee.

The seamen were near giddy. Some of them were exhausted and giddy, and one-by-one they began fainting: first one, then the other; sixteen in all. They were laughing one moment, then their eyes turned back and they floated to the floor. The town doctor, Dr. Carroll Keene, treated them all. They all recovered. The Rev. Steve Smith tended those who needed spiritual help or prayer.

Bernie stood in the doorway and may have taken in the scene but did not remember it. He did not really remember even leaving the CG 36500. He was onboard one moment, then sitting on his bunk inside the life station the next, bending over to take off his boots. Chief Bill Woodman was talking to him. That was the first thing he remembered and he told Woodman he felt okay and wanted some coffee and they walked to the galley.

Webber could not believe the commotion. His crew was there, all safe and sound. Cluff came up to him and shook his hand, said he never thought that he'd see Bernie again and then spoke quietly about how upset the officers were about the whole radio thing. There had been talk of charges and court martial, Cluff told Webber. Though he thought that would not happen now. Webber walked over to a table and grabbed a Cushman's doughnut. He talked with his crew, shook hands with a few of the mariners and with Sybert. Flashbulbs were everywhere. Already there was talk about awards and medals.

Then Bernie headed back up to his bunk. He crawled into a cozy bed and heaped on blankets and either fell into a deep sleep or passed out. It was hard to say.

Bernie slept for eighteen hours straight and when he awoke, he was sure he had dreamed it all.

Then he saw puddles of water on the floor. A trail of wet, soggy dollar bills led to an open drawer. Inside were more wet bills, wadded and crumpled. More than $200.

In the night, while Webber slept, the crew had come one-by-one and emptied their wallets into the Coast Guardsman's drawer. And he knew it was real.

Then and only then did John Stello, the fisherman who had told Bernie to get lost rather than shoot the bar, call Miriam.

"Hey Miriam," Stello said. "Did you know Bernie's a hero?"

"What for?" Miriam asked. Stello told her, and none of them had any idea how such good news was the harbinger of a strange and different future.

Those rescued from the
Pendleton swarm off the
CG 36500 in Chatham.
**Photo courtesy of the Orleans
Historical Society**

The crew of the CG 36500—Bernard Webber, Andrew Fitzgerald, Richard Livesey, and
Irving Maske—after the rescue.

Nineteen

CLEANUP

February 1952
Off Cape Cod

Anyone who could be saved had been saved. A mariner's next thoughts turn to salvage.

Here, by far, Bushnell and his half-ship of the *Fort Mercer* fared the best. Some cargo remained whole in its tanks and the half-ship itself had commercial value. The stern section was riding pretty clear and free of danger. The twelve men who stayed on the stern section with Bushnell were comfortable enough that they chose to remain there even after the seas had quieted. A tug took the section under tow and brought it to a Newport, Rhode Island, shipyard.

The *Pendleton*'s bow was boarded by the Coast Guard. Only one body was found on board. Herman G. Gatlin, a seaman, had entered the cargo area of the bow and covered himself in sawdust as insulation against the cold. He had died of exposure. All the other men apparently were washed overboard, though it never was exactly clear how they met their deaths, and when. The bow was eventually towed away and sold for scrap iron.

Days after the disaster, the Jacobs ladder still was tied to the rail of the *Pendleton's* stern half. It is visible snaking down the side of the hull.

Not so the stern. For year's, the stern of the *Pendleton* served as a sort of local landmark, a reminder of both the tragedy and the triumphant rescue. A big storm in 1978 submerged the stern section so it became a hazard to navigation. A contractor carved it into small pieces that sank to the bottom. One diving guide says the *Pendleton* pieces comprise the best artificial reef for scuba diving on Cape Cod. In theory, the stern of the *Pendleton* had not been salvaged at all. In reality, Bernie knew, a mischievous band of mariners from Chatham no doubt had visited the wreck several times once the weather cleared. The "Chatham pirates" were a throwback to the old days of shipwrecking where whole clans lived on the proceeds of salvaged goods. Webber knew the men had been out there, but he and the other Coasties were careful not to catch their hometown friends. So they picked up a ton or two of bronze and a few galley items. This was harmless stuff. He knew Harold Claflin was one of the pirates and rumors around town were that he had scored the most treasured souvenir of the *Pendleton*, the ship's clock. Well, God bless him then, Bernie thought. The *Pendleton* had brought enough sadness. Let it make someone happy.

Just as the *Fort Mercer* bow posed the most problems during the rescue effort, so too did it during cleanup. The bow section had turned-turtle and would have certainly killed the officers had they remained there.

But then it would not do the obliging thing and sink all the way. It bobbed about in the waters, half-sunk, half-floating. The Coast Guard quickly declared it a hazard to navigation. But the permission of the ship owners were needed in order to destroy the bow. The owners would not give the green light until a salvage tug, the *Foundation Josephine*, inspected the wreckage to see whether salvage was possible. The cutter *Unimak* spent a long night attempting to keep track of the bow, and when the salvage tug drew near, the *Unimak* officers asked the salvage experts what their thoughts were.

"For God's sakes, man, sink her!" said the officer on the salvage tug. "I'll take the responsibility myself."

The *Unimak* closed in on the hulk and opened fire with 40-mm cannon, expecting to see the wreck sink or explode from its remaining cargoes of oil and kerosene.

Instead, the bow section continued to float and to flaunt the Coast Guard. The kerosene would ignite briefly, burn, and then blow out from the winds. The cannon rounds were piercing the bow section, but not in places where it reduced buoyancy. The Coast Guard then unlimbered its big 5-inch gun and fired on the hulk. The bigger gun brought no bigger results.

Frustrated, Commander Frank M. McCabe told the crew to ready depth charges. McCabe had served during the war on anti-submarine patrol and knew what underwater explosions could do to the buoyancy of sealed metal spaces. A depth charge essentially was a barrel full of high explosives rigged to go off underwater.

McCabe would fire the depth charges using a K-gun that hurled the barrels away from the cutter. He gave the order to pass the bow section at full speed so the cutter itself would not be harmed by the blast.

The run went perfectly. The depth charges ignited as planned. The concussion rocked the bow section and sent plumes of water into the air. But the bow itself sat there stubbornly, unmoved. McCabe gave the order to make another run; they were readying it when the bow teetered, swayed, then sank beneath the sea.

When the salvage was done, the formal Marine Board of Investigation began. These courtlike proceedings called witnesses and reached conclusions about the ship and anyone who acted improperly to cause the wreck.

Both boards came in with the same verdict. T-2s were flawed ships. No one acted improperly, though the ships might have been loaded a bit more evenly. The crack arrestors would have held in quiet water, but not in rough water.

The American Bureau of Shipping, the technical organization responsible for certifying the soundness of vessels, recommended that all T-2s be fitted with four more crack arrestors. Still, there was not the presumption that this would make the ships whole. The crack arrestors were installed to keep the ships afloat so that the crew and officers had time to steer to port or rescue.

No one suggested that the ships be scrapped. Not the officers, not the engineers, not the crewmen. Their suggestions for safety were in the context of when this happens again.

When this happens again, you should have radios on the stern end. When this happens again, you should have ladders from the bridge to the deck. When this happens again, some deck officers should be stationed aft with knowledge of blinkers and code. When this happens again, reliable emergency power should be available on the bow.

No one wanted to see the ships scrapped; no one could afford that. The country and the economy needed oil and energy, and the men needed jobs. There were always risks at sea. They were accustomed to oversized risk.

So what if you could die by fire *and* ice. Hell, they were tanker men. If you made that initial choice, then the possibility of your ship breaking in two was kind of an incremental risk to the job description.

The T-2s kept sailing, as did the men.

Twenty

THE GOADING SLUR

February 19, 1952 to March 31, 1952
Chatham

*W**e killed a man back there.* The thought struck Bernie even before he and the CG 36500 had reached homeport. The rest of the crew felt some variation of this.

Perhaps it was because Bernie was looking into the eyes of Tiny Myers as the man died. Perhaps if the crewman had simply been lost, he would not feel this way. Perhaps if the boat had not surged forward as it had and struck Myers, these thoughts would have lessened or disappeared entirely.

They did not. Bernie could not get it out of his head. It was not that we lost a man back there. We *killed* a man back there.

No one else was viewing it that way. In fact, the Coast Guard rescuers were hailed nationwide, on the front pages of newspapers, on radio, and on the new televisions people were now buying everywhere.

And while there were no shortage of heroes, the attention naturally focused on CG 36500, the little boat that went out through thunderous surf and mountainous waves to the huge ship and miraculously saved so many men.

As this edition of a Boston newspaper illustrates, the rescue was headline news around the country—and the world. Photo courtesy of the Orleans Historical Society

Bangs and his crew would have had the glory, Bernie thought, if they had not been sent about like a ping-pong ball that night. That crew had spent far more time out in the storm and the cold than Bernie. They were every bit as heroic as Bernie and his crew but just not, in a strange way, as fortunate.

Chief Bangs was depressed now and blamed himself for not rescuing the man on the bow of the *Pendleton*. But had they not sent him back for that one man, Bangs and his crew would have reached the *Pendleton* stern and been the big heroes. Or you could look to the cutters too, the *Fort Mercer* stern rescue, or the incredible work Kiley did in his little Monomoy surfboat.

But attention naturally focused on Bernie—the attention of the public and the brass. The Coast Guard needed some heroes, certainly, to keep up its image and funding. But the *Pendleton* rescue did seem near-miraculous to everyone, even admirals. It was not long after news of the wreck emerged that the commandant of the Coast Guard fired off a telegram congratulating Bernie and his crew.

A few days after the rescue, Cluff called Bernie into his office, smiling. He held a phone in his hand and said something like, "Here Bernie, there's a call for you."

Bernie took the call and greeted Captain Morine of Coast Guard headquarters. Morine got right down to the good news and said something like: "The Coast Guard is awarding you the Gold Lifesaving Medal and your crew the Silver Life Saving Medal, son. What do you think of that?"

Bernie did not have to think about it at all.

"I think it *stinks*," he shot back to the officer. "For whatever reasoning it was determined I should receive the gold the same should apply to them. They were there; the risks were the same."

"Are you serious?" the captain replied, and Webber shot back something roughly like this: "I certainly am. And if my crew doesn't get the gold, I don't want it either."

There was a long pause on the end of the line. Cluff looked like an animated cartoon figure he was so flustered by Webber's conduct.

"I understand," the captain said at last. "So be it."

And so that was settled. Kiley would win the gold and his Monomoy boat crewmen the silver for their efforts at the bow of the *Fort Mercer*. But the CG 36500 crew was to be the gold-medal crew, not the gold-medal coxswain.

Still, an interior voice whispered to Bernie almost daily: *We killed a man back there.* Yes, he was happy that he had saved so many. But it was the one loss that haunted him. Outside the immediate crew, no one else felt this way. That was obvious. But in a culture where you had to go out but you did not have to come back, it wasn't a far jump to wonder why you left someone out there. There was the culture of courage that propelled men out to sea and there was also the cruel culture of the "goading slur" for those rescuers who failed or were less than perfect specimens of the lifesaving species.

So Webber felt the goading slur. Only it was not coming from his colleagues or superiors or the townspeople. It was coming from Bernie himself. *We killed a man back there,* the interior voice said. He could not shake the feeling of guilt and failure.

Perhaps that was the worse curse of the rescue. It was not to be the only one.

Twenty-One

STRANGE WATERS

April to December 1952
Chatham

Bernie Webber became the poster boy for the U.S. Coast Guard that year. He received not only the Gold Lifesaving Medal, the highest honor within his service, but the American Legion Medal of Valor as well.

He was constantly on the road in the months after the rescue. There was the award ceremony in Washington, D.C. There were banquets in Boston. Kiwanis, Jaycees, Rotary clubs: you name it, Bernie spoke there. He was humble and understated. He did not have to be anything more. The story was well known in the land about the little boat that could and pulled off the most impossible rescue of all time.

And it was about this time that Bernie noted a change in how he was treated by peers and officers alike. He wanted nothing more than to blend back into the culture that had formed him. He wanted to be one of the guys again. This was a very collegial business, this lifesaving craft. You worked as a team with a set of cultural norms that you had to live up to.

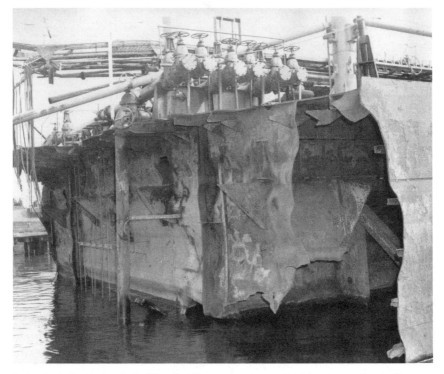

In dry dock, the broken hull of the *Fort Mercer* stern is examined for clues as to why the tanker broke in two.

Most heroes, from Achilles to those who raised the American flag on Iwo Jima, find themselves in this odd state of suspension between old worlds and new. In ancient Greek mythology, Achilles was part-man, part-god but fully a part of neither group. The gods would not take him to Olympus and the mortals were reminded by the hero's presence of their own shortcomings. So too can it be for modern heroes who find that it is after their act of bravery when courage is needed most.

It wasn't as if Bernie were shunned at the Coast Guard lifeboat station in Chatham. But it was, well, *awkward* now.

Bangs essentially ran the station. And Bangs still felt immense guilt about not rescuing the man from the *Pendleton* bow. Others began interpreting any action of Bernie's as putting on airs. Still others thought wrongly that he was making money from the rescue from all the speeches he made and all the articles that were written about him.

Then, too, there was the embarrassment of those at the station who Bernie had wanted as his crew members. He was blessed by the "volunteer" crew, but where had the regulars been? The "first team?" Where had they been when the order was given to take the CG 36500 across the Chatham Bar?

Bernie did not "call them out." He did not have to. Everyone knew who they were. And every time they saw Bernie, they were reminded of what they had not done. They felt their own "goading slur."

It was odd how this worked. He was the same guy. He wasn't making money on this.

Then there were questions raised about the rescue—questions that were picky and petty by any standard, but hurtful to Bernie given his state of mind.

Why had they not brought in Tiny Myers's body? Some asked that. The answer would have been obvious had anyone been there. There were more men in the water who could be saved.

But Cluff and Sybert, the chief engineer of the *Pendleton*, had cooked up a seemingly harmless story, what seemed at the time like a benevolent lie. They told the press and Myers's family that Tiny had been the last man down, that Tiny had been a hero himself standing on the last rung hoisting people into the boat with no regard to his own safety. The men had not perjured themselves. Cluff and Sybert testified accurately during the Marine Board of Investigation.

But the public story was that Myers was the last man down. If so, even if he was dead, why did Bernie not just pick up the body? It wasn't a small deal. You brought back bodies if you could.

Webber would not give the real reason; he could not say that the rescue was still underway and that there were still live men in the water who needed rescue. He refrained from saying that for more than five decades out of respect to the Myers family and to Myers himself. Of course, even if Myers had been the last man down, this was still a ridiculous criticism. Why did he not bring back the body of the thirty-third man? How he got thirty-two men into a boat rated for twenty was the real question. Still, it took a little chunk out of the hero's armor. It brought him down a peg, if you wanted to play like that. And some folks did.

The other point was the radar. Webber said he found the hulk by himself with no compass and no help. Then he found Old Harbor himself with no assistance and no help. Some of his critics wondered, wasn't that pushing it just a bit too far? Did he not in fact follow radar instructions? What else could explain the rescue? Why did he claim to have navigated in this manner when it was clear the radar had guided him in?

Again, Webber was handicapped in giving a clear answer to this because of exaggerations by Cluff of the radar's helpfulness. Radar was expensive, and Cluff wanted more of it. He spread the word that the radar had been of great help and the well-meant sophistry crept into the folklore of the rescue. Radar became a hero in the rescue as well.

In fact, no one, including Cluff, stated in the formal Marine Board of Investigation that radar helped Webber at any time. It was sketchy technology back then. The specialist at the screen was there to repair the radar, not run it. It did seem as if the radar helped locate the *Pendleton*, which was an important feat. But it was far from a star that day.

Of none of these things would Bernie Webber speak to directly. He did not want to undermine Cluff. He did not want to undermine the story about Myers's heroism. Bernie had done what he had done. He had never felt particularly brave or special. If he talked about it at all, he said it was just good luck and the work of the Lord. He had been following the values of the Coast Guard, a service whose men and values he loved and which now seemed for some reason to be turning against him. It was an egalitarian culture, and there is much within egalitarian cultures to be cherished. But there is also something in the culture that does not love a hero. At least not for long. Heroes get torn down so they are equal again, mere mortals. Or they are cast out.

Bernie was cast out. Or cast himself out. He transferred out to Masachi thinking that would end it. He was with his mentor now, on board the CG 83388 out of the Coast Guard base at Woods Hole, second officer in command.

But even then the problems followed. He would be on duty, then get a call from the brass. He was needed at a speech here, an interview there. How could he be Masachi's number two when he could not be dependably relied on to be there? He *wanted* to be there, but the brass would not let him stay put.

No one would let him stay put, in fact. His crews and his commanding officers always seemed to be testing him. Always, it seemed, they wanted to see if the hero was cracked up to be what he was said to be.

At one level, Webber did not help things. There was that voice, his interior goading slur, that no doubt magnified any words of outside doubt or critique. Webber did not think of himself a hero and the guilt over Myers's death was always with him.

On another level, Webber *had* changed. He was no longer the young man looking for guidance. He'd gotten guidance. He had followed it. He had done what he thought was right and what he had to do. He had his code from the Coast Guard. So he could deal with it. He wasn't like David Atkins of Provincetown who in 1870 felt he had to redeem himself through another act of courage, to rid himself of the goading slur. Webber did not have to prove his courage at all.

But he did. Four times before he retired he would show great courage in service—even if the service did not at times return the favor.

Twenty-Two

THE THIRTY-THIRD MAN

March 1955
Chatham

Bernie Webber spent two years serving out of the Coast Guard base at Woods Hole with Masachi on the CG 83388, a larger search and rescue vessel. Masachi was officer in charge and his old mentor, Alvin E. Newcomb, was the executive officer of the entire base. Whatever troubles came his way, even the public relations assignments by the brass, these two men had Bernie's back. They were touchstones to the core values of the Coast Guard.

But both were near retirement age in 1954 and Webber transferred back to Chatham in July of that year. Miriam and Bernie had a son by that time. With help from Bernie's carpenter father-in-law, the Webber's built a small house. They were among family now, with some of them literally next door. Webber truly felt like a native Cape Codder.

And he could also work the CG 36500 again. It is not an exaggeration to say that Webber felt a mystical attraction to the little rescue boat. Damned if he could put his finger on it. He knew one boat should be pretty much like another. But there was something about the CG 36500, and there had been almost from the start, that was close to love at first glance. It was silly, he knew, but there it was.

And there *he* was on a typical March day in Cape Cod back at Chatham. Out at sea, the ocean swell ran very high but it was smooth and broad in between the peaks of waves. At times, Webber thought of them as hills of salt water.

He could see his old nemesis, the Chatham Bar. Breakers were forming there as the tide ran out. Those big swells rose up, met the outgoing tide, and crashed in the shallows of the bar. Even on a normal day, those big rollers could make the bar unsafe.

Word this day had gone out to the Chatham fishing fleet about the building bad conditions. The fishermen took the bar seriously. As conditions worsened, they came home, crossing the bar without incident.

Only Joe Stapleton, a quiet man who fished alone, was still out there. It was no big deal. He could still make it in if he was careful. In the watchtower, near evening, the Coasties sighted a boat just northeast of the *Pollock Rip* lightship and soon, as it drew closer, everyone knew it was Joe. He had a green boat. Plus, they could tell by the way the exhaust fumes came from the engine that this was Joe's boat.

Nothing much was happening. There was no cause for alarm. On a whim, Webber asked Chief Ralph Ormsby if he could take the CG 36500 out to meet Stapleton and escort him back in. Ormsby thought about it for a while. Everything was low key. Boredom was a real enemy some days. Sure, why not, he said finally.

Webber's crew ambled down to a truck that took them to the CG 36500 and they rowed out in a dory to the lifeboat. The sun was at about the height of the lighthouse and Chatham radiated its beauty back to the crew. It was that sort of raking light of evening when the landscape seemed to illuminate from within.

They clambered into the CG 36500 and cranked the ninety-horse-power Sterling until it caught and then coughed white smoke into the cold air. They moved leisurely out toward the bar through Old Harbor enjoying the evening sun-lit scenery. Once near Morris Island, they could see the ocean and there was Joe's boat, chugging surely along. He would probably beat them to the bar with the progress he was making.

That was at least the assumption when Bernie stopped the CG 36500 on the landside of the bar. The breaking seas on the bar seemed even more evident now. He expected to see Joe's boat come in high on a wave and cross the bar. The bar was bad, but Joe was an experienced hand. It could be done.

Nothing. Webber waited another minute, then radioed the station. Had anyone seen Joe crossing the bar? Negative came the reply. Then word came from men on the lookout tower. They had seen Joe start to cross the bar, but had lost sight of him in the surf. Was he not on the far side? The safe side?

Webber revved the engine and waited no longer. He and the crew both knew what had to be done now. The CG 36500 turned again toward the breaking waves of the shallows of the Chatham Bar.

She rode up those waves without incident this time and gracefully slipped down the silk-like far side of the turbulence into the high but gentle ocean rollers.

No sign of Joe, no sign of the boat. Had Joe gotten by them in the harbor somehow? No chance, Webber thought. He called back to the station. It was getting darker. He left the CG 36500 in gear at low speed so Bernie and the crew were carried in slow meandering circles. Bernie's attention was on the radio now, and his hand was not even on the wheel. The CG 36500 was in effect steering herself. Where was Joe's boat? Had they seen Joe's boat?

Nothing. No sign. That was the word back. The boat was not on the ocean side or the harbor side. There was no boat.

Webber and the crew continued to scan the ocean as the CG 36500, driverless, meandered about. Someone thought they saw a dark shape in front and Bernie grabbed the wheel now, edging the little boat in closer.

There in the water, just 3 feet under the surface, lay Joe Stapleton's boat. Her bow bobbed just that far down, her stern pointing to the bottom, suspended just so. The sunken boat would rise and fall with each wave but neither sink wholly nor surface.

Bernie thought to himself that Joe was trapped below. There was nothing they could do for him now. They had arrived too late. Stapleton was dead.

It was growing ever darker. Bernie radioed in the bad news and asked them: Did they want him to grapple the wreck and try to bring it in over the bar? Or mark the hulk and handle it tomorrow in daytime?

He was fully engaged in the conversation and the instructions and his hand was off the wheel again as the CG 36500 circled about at lowest throttle; then, through some effect of wave or wind, the boat broke its circle and moved south a bit. Webber did not think to correct the course. It made no difference. He could find the sunken boat easily enough. They just had to decide what they wanted him to do. It was nearly dark now. Bring the boat and the body in, or wait until daylight?

"Hey," a crew member said. "There's something in the water up ahead."

Webber came back to command and grabbed the wheel, then sped the boat up. But when they got there it was only a wooden bait tub, probably from Joe's boat. Off in the distance floated another dark object and Bernie now headed for that one, perhaps a bit more of the fishing vessel's debris.

Joe Stapleton floated silently in the water beside the CG 36500. He did not say a word. He had a life jacket clasped to him and the big swells picked him up and laid him down like a cork on the water. His eyes were wide open—frozen in a wild stare is how Bernie thought of it. Stapleton showed no sign of life, no awareness that Bernie and his crew were there.

They grabbed him with their boathook then and hoisted him over the side of the CG 36500. The body was limp, dead. Then Stapleton's hand moved and he released his grip on the life jacket he had clung to. The crew scrambled to. They took him down below to the forward cabin, took off their outerwear and piled it on him. They rubbed his body down as Bernie turned the CG 36500 back to cross the bar again.

They arrived back at the Fish Pier and an ambulance rushed Stapleton to the hospital. He stayed there for a few days, was treated for exposure, and was back at the Fish Pier later in the week.

When he saw Bernie, he would nod but say nothing. Each time, there would be a nod but no words. It's how fishermen are, Bernie thought. He found it to be true a lot of the time among seamen. When a life and death situation had developed and passed, you just let it be. You didn't talk about it.

Bernie found that useful himself at times. How was he to explain the CG 36500? In his mind, the CG 36500 had done all the work. He was not hallucinating this. His hand had been off the wheel. The little boat with no navigating hand took them first to the wreck, then to the bait bucket, and then to Joe.

Was it spooky? Religious? Webber wasn't sure. That was between Joe, the boat, and God, as far as he was concerned. But the incident only increased Bernie's feeling about the CG 36500, that she was special, near mystical. He also, secretly, referred to Stapleton as "the thirty-third man." He had saved thirty-two off the *Pendleton*. Now, the CG 36500 had saved the thirty-third—a man who should have died but did not.

He wasn't silly about it. He didn't think the CG 36500 was holy. She didn't talk to him. But there was something about her that summed up all that was good about the Coast Guard and tradition. And he was not a religious zealot, but he could not help but think that God had a hand in all this somehow: the *Pendleton*, Stapleton, the CG 36500. The boat was blessed, let's put it that way. And that made what he had to do later one of the hardest tasks of his life.

Twenty-Three

FIRES ON THE BEACH

Chatham

Always, even years later, Bernie Webber was the poster boy for Coast Guard heroism. This meant speeches, yes, but at times it also meant high-profile assignments. The Coast Guard was developing new lifeboats to replace the 36-footers. And the brass wanted Bernie to test out these new 44-footers.

He was of a mixed mind about the matter from the start. His allegiance was to the 36-footers, to the CG 36500. Had they not proven themselves for decades under the most severe circumstances?

And he did not really comprehend the purpose of the new 44-footers at first. He ran them on trials and was unimpressed. The brass, expecting an endorsement from Bernie, found instead a long list of complaints.

This resistance to progress was as much a tradition in the Coast Guard as was change and innovation. During World War II, one part of the Coast Guard pioneered the use of helicopters as rescue craft. But another, more politically potent part of the Coast Guard, the fixed-wing flight division, shut down the rotary boys for years—long after choppers should have been deployed as standard rescue practice. Helicopters may or may not have been able to help in the *Fort Mercer-Pendleton* rescues. No one knew, for there weren't any available.

And once the helicopters came, there was still more resistance to using them appropriately. The first choppers carried an awkward sling device, which was so cumbersome that an American astronaut, drilled in how to use the sling, was nearly lost at sea once landed because he could not make the sling work. A simple basket device was far more effective, yet it took years to implement it.

The same held true for such innovations as rescue swimmers. Coast Guard helicopter rescue crews were tightly bound operations, each man playing a role in a chopper rescue. But if the victims below were too cold to swim to a rescue basket or even to grasp it, then the men in the helicopters could do little. The Navy had figured that out years ago during carrier work. The Coast Guard, bound by tradition, rejected and resisted the concept.

This sort of change was opposed by men who thought the old ways were best and saw innovation as an erosion of values and tradition. You could say that Bernie Webber was a man like that. Certainly, he had not liked a lot of the change he had seen lately in the Coast Guard. The lifeboat men were being de-emphasized now that the choppers were around. And this new 44-footer would destroy his last link to the old days. What were they going to do with the old 36-footers? Sell them off?

And yet, he knew this had to happen. The CG 36500 was beautiful and always would be. But he thought back to the rescue, the original one. That little Sterling 90-horsepower gasoline engine had gotten them there and back. But it had also failed them so often in rough seas. The new 44s had twin diesel engines, each with 180 horsepower. The 36s had one propeller; the 44s had two screws so they could maneuver on a dime.

The 36500 had a compass and a radio. The 44s had a compass, several radios, a depth finder, and even radar. The 36500 was rated for twenty rescued. The 44s could handle far more, and in heated quarters with seatbelts. The 36 footers were self-righting, but so were the 44s—and the pilot quarters were enclosed. The 36-footers had wooden hulls; the 44s were solid steel.

They asked Bernie to take the 44 out again in April 1962 and run it up and down the Eastern seaboard and test it in the roughest weather he could. They had made some modifications to her. Would he give it a try?

Webber took the prototype out to sea. He took the ship into any weather he could find. He did long, heavy tows at high speeds in open water. He did his best to roll the 44 over.

He had to say it. Nothing much bothered this boat. Would the Coast Guard be better off with the 36-footers or the new 44s? He had to go with the 44-footers and told the brass that. It was not what he wanted to say but what he had to say, because it was true.

This was a death sentence for the CG 36500, he knew. They would get rid of the 36-footers soon. What he did not know was that they would burn the sturdy old boats on the beach. There was a mass burning of the boats at the water's edge near the Chatham cut-through. They just beached and burned them right there. Then they scavenged the ashes for brass fittings.

For Bernie, it was a heartbreaking sight. That is how he thought of it: heartbreak. The CG 36500 was not in that first batch to burn, but he knew her time was coming.

Twenty-Four

OLDSTYLE

January 1962
Chatham

E ven before then, he felt dated. The burning of the 36-footers was just one symptom of the change that had overtaken him. The Coast Guard was modernizing and those who resisted change risked ridicule.

Take the old Lyle Gun and the Breeches Buoy rigs, which are of nineteenth-century origin. Ships of sail would drift onto Cape Cod shores hundreds of yards from the beach. No one could row out to get them through the surf, and the ships were soon pounded to pieces by the breakers. In an attempt to save their lives, the crew and officers would climb the sailing masts.

From shore, if you knew what you were doing, you could take a Lyle Gun (which was a small cannon, really), load black powder down its barrel, place a metal projectile tied to a line, and fire the cannon off to send the projectile and line over the wrecked ship.

The stranded crew could then drag more lines to the boat and secure them to the mast. One line carried a strange looking setup, which was in its essence a set of very large canvas "breeches," or pants, tied to a buoy and to the rope. A crew member would scramble into the breeches part of the contraption and be held there securely. Then through a system of pulleys and lines, the men on shore would haul him over the waves and to safety.

The concept sounded unlikely, but the combination of the Lyle Gun and the Breeches Buoy saved hundreds of lives over the years. The Coast Guard still trained its men to use the technique. But these days, it seemed fitted only as a good show for tourists and an example of the bad old days. These were the good old days of helicopters, after all.

The Coast Guard brass surveyed those on the Cape. Bernie was by this time (1960) officer in charge at Chatham. Did everyone agree they could dispose of Lyle Gun training? Most of the Cape's Coast Guard leaders said yes; Bernie said no. You might need the technique, he said. Choppers are great, but there are some instances where you still might need the gun and the breeches setup. And besides, it's a good exercise for the men. It builds teamwork and it links them back to the tradition and dedication of the original surf men.

Webber was widely ridiculed and near officially classified an old-timer and worse, a has-been. The Lyle Gun training was stopped, with just one crew and rig left on the Cape. Bernie could feel his love for the old ways and the old Coast Guard just leaking from him. Ten years after his rescue he seemed all but washed up.

Still, when the call came for a Provincetown rescue, the old training kicked in. On January 16, 1962 the fishing vessel *Margaret Rose* had run aground on an offshore shoal nearly 200 yards from shore. A 40-mile-per-hour wind pushed up seas that rocked the fishing vessel and crashed down upon her.

The first reports of the distress came at around 3:30 a.m. and the new Coast Guard was on the spot. A helicopter was there by 4 a.m. hovering over the *Margaret Rose*, ready to lift the seven men aboard to safety. But the ship was rocking so to and fro below that the chopper could not lower a basket without running afoul of whipping lines and masts.

This was nothing for Bernie to worry about. Race Point was at the wrist of Cape Cod. He was down in Chatham at the elbow of the Cape, miles away. The Race Point Lifeboat Station was right there.

A motor lifeboat was sent to the scene of the *Margaret Rose* but the crew found they could not get close enough to the vessel to lend any aid. The water was too rough and too shallow to make a decent approach. Race Point sent a DUKW, an amphibious vehicle, to do the job. But it broke down as it traveled over the dunes and was out of commission.

So a little after 4 a.m., the call went out to Chatham Lifeboat Station. Boston search and rescue headquarters gave Bernie a briefing on the situation. He was ordered to speed to Provincetown and do whatever he could to help.

Webber acknowledged the order and had one request, almost as an afterthought. Could Boston call the Cape Cod Canal Lifeboat Station and have them send a Lyle Gun and a Breeches Buoy to P-town? It was the last station on Cape Cod to maintain the equipment.

Webber then grabbed two crewmen, Daniel Davidson, an engine-man first class, and Wayne Chapuis, a seaman. They dressed as warmly as they could and climbed into their station's DUKW. The amphibious vehicle was open to the January air and the men became chilled during the 35-mile drive to Provincetown.

Once there, Webber could see the scene was little changed. The chopper hovered nearby helplessly and men stood on the beach watching. Out on the *Margaret Rose*, the seven crewmen had climbed up the fishing vessel's masts to avoid being washed away. The boat herself was awash, with waves breaking over the deck and pounding the hull to pieces.

The Lyle Gun had not arrived. Webber could do only one thing. He drove the DUKW over the beach and directly into the water. The clumsy vehicle was lifted up by the first wave it hit and then nosedived down the far side of the wave, just as another wave rolled right in on top of it.

Webber's vehicle was swamped and sunk right there. They were only about 100 feet offshore, and still 500 feet from the wreck—and the water was not deep. So the men made it back to shore fine. But the DUKW was going nowhere. Only its windshield showed above water.

Soaked and freezing, Webber trekked back to the beach and found that the equipment from the Canal station had arrived. Now what? He had been an advocate of the Lyle Gun training, but that's all he'd ever done: trained. He'd never actually ever performed a Breeches Buoy rescue. He did not know anyone who had. It was something you read about and drilled for, just for the drill. He knew the theory and knew the equipment, but he had fired a Lyle Gun only once. And that was a practical joke to scare their mailman in Chatham (which worked fine).

But this was no joke. It was nearly light now and Webber could see the wreck was in bad shape. Plus, there was always the danger of fire. The seas could hit the batteries in the vessel and that meant explosion would surely follow.

He was nervous; he was abrupt. He was a low-key leader and it was not in his nature to take command like this. But now he barked out commands to men who weren't his men, hoping the men thought he knew what he was doing.

He lined the men up on the beach, told them not to ask questions but to just remember what he said and then follow orders. Then Webber walked down the line and pointed at one, then another. "You, lee whip. You, weather whip. You, lee whip. You, weather whip." So he went down the line until the men were divided into two groups. But for what, they were not sure.

Then Webber and the men brought the Lyle Gun down to the beach and pointed it toward the *Margaret Rose*. Webber loaded two ounces of powder down the barrel of the Lyle Gun, then he hesitated. He tried to remember whether that was the standard charge. Then he put in two more ounces, just to make sure.

Then he tied a line onto a steel projectile and put the projectile into the cannon barrel. He attached a firing clip to a blank cartridge that would set the powder off and grabbed the lanyard that would trigger it all. He checked to see whether the cannon was pointed correctly and then said aloud: "God, make this shot good, Amen."

BLAM!

The Lyle Gun jumped clear of the ground, lurched, fell backward and upside down into the sand, such was the force of the double load of powder.

But Webber could hear the whistle of the projectile in the air. He could see it, too. To him, it looked as if it were heading toward Boston. He lost sight of it and no one was sure exactly where it landed.

No one much cared. For while the cannon was overloaded and the projectile was out of sight, the line itself was now settling over the wreck in a feathery drape, just as it was supposed to. The fishermen were able to grab it and haul on it. The slim line carried in a heavier line with instructions for the fishermen. They were to rig lines on the masts far above the water and the deck.

On the beach, the Coasties anchored all the lines to a jeep. After some fast hauling back and forth, the men on the vessel and the men on the beach had constructed a type of very large pulley-driven clothes line. Haul one way, and the clothes went out your window. Haul the other way and the clothes came back in. It was the same principle. Only they were not hauling clothes; they were hauling men.

On the shore, the Coast Guardsmen attached the Breeches Buoy to one line. The men Bernie had designated "lee whips" pulled one way; the "weather whips" pulled the other. The buoy apparatus quickly reached the masts of the fishing vessel and the first man slipped into the breeches and was quickly carried to safety.

Back and forth, the lines went. The lee whips and the weather whips moved the men one by one from the danger of the masts to the safety of the shore. Six times they did this, but the seventh time was anything but lucky.

The seas picked up and the wind rocked the *Margaret Rose*. It was difficult to maintain tension in the lines as the vessel rocked.

Still, the canvas breeches were whipped out to the last man. He clambered into the contraption, sitting down into the canvas pants. Then everyone heard a sharp crack. The mast just snapped clean in two. The man fell with the mast into the water, still in the breeches. He was quickly swept along the beach struggling with the lines, the apparatus, the wind, and the waves.

The Coasties were running by then. The men from Bernie's crew, Davidson and Chapius, immediately ran down the beach. It was as if they were in the old Etheridge days now. They had tried boats, and that had failed. They had tried the gun, and that had failed. There was nothing now to do but swim for him. Complete old school.

And that was what they did. They plunged into the icy January water, reached the man, cut him loose of the lines and breeches, and swam him to shore. He was still alive when the batteries aboard the *Margaret Rose* exploded and set the vessel afire.

Bernie looked up into the sky and the helicopter was still hovering nearby. Well, sometimes has-beens still had their day, he thought. Sometimes the old ways worked.

But he knew then that the old Coast Guard was gone. That this was an exception and no longer the rule.

If he had any doubts about that, the next surprise would cure them.

Twenty-Five

"THE COLDEST THING"

Woods Hole

Webber left Chatham station for duties that eventually found him officer in charge of the Coast Guard cutter *Point Banks*. It was pleasant enough duty. The Coast Guard brass occasionally would use Bernie as a poster boy, but that was less and less the case. The *Point Banks* operated out of Woods Hole on the Cape, so he was close to his old friends and his family. By then, Bernie and Miriam had three children.

But Webber had decided it was time to move on so he filed for retirement on September 1, 1965. He was coasting out aboard the *Point Banks* but still working hard in late April 1965. The 82-foot cutter and its crew had been on a two-week patrol and the weather had been stormy, save for the last day. Bernie was a senior chief boatswain's mate now and he backed the engines down as he eased the *Point Banks* into Woods Hole.

A seaman eagerly jumped ashore with a line to secure the cutter. They all felt a sense of relief as Bernie killed the engines. Webber intended to give the seven-man crew the maximum liberty. They had worked hard and deserved it.

154

As they were leaving the cutter, though, a message arrived from First Coast Guard District headquarters. It said simply, "Proceed to Coast Guard Base Boston to receive a new Boston Whaler."

This made no sense to Bernie. A Boston Whaler was an open boat that easily could be hauled behind a truck—or a car, for that matter. He was sharp with the dispatcher.

"There's no reason you can't put a boat like that on a truck and send it down to Woods Hole. What's the deal, making me bring a cutter 80 miles to Boston just to pick up a boat? We just got in off patrol. You're messing up my crew's liberty."

The dispatcher cut him off.

"Senior chief, those are your orders. Proceed to Boston immediately."

Webber had no choice. The liberty was cancelled. The cutter refueled and sailed north; it transited the Cape Cod Canal and crept toward Boston. By 7:15 that evening they reached the Boston base and it looked deserted. Webber was finishing log entries when a lieutenant came down the pier.

"Listen, senior chief, they want you to put on your dress blues and be prepared to meet the press," the lieutenant said.

This baffled Bernie. They'd used him like this before, but not in a long time. Why were they trotting out their local hero? He said simply to the officer: "What for, sir?"

"Haven't you heard?" the lieutenant said, a note of disbelief in his voice.

Bernie bit: "Heard what?"

The lieutenant smiled back at him with what he thought was good news.

"Well, you fellows are going to Vietnam."

"You've got to be kidding," Webber said.

"No, you're going to Vietnam," the lieutenant said. "So get yourself and your crew into dress blues and get ready to meet the press."

155

Bernie was in a hurry all right, but it wasn't to get dressed. He got to a phone and quickly called Miriam.

"You better sit down," he said. And he told her he wanted her to hear the news about Vietnam before she heard it on the news or from someone else.

Webber could have kept his retirement papers filed. They would not have deployed him if he kept firm to his decision to retire on September 1, which was just four months away.

But that also meant he would be sending his crew into a combat zone with a new officer in charge. They would have little time together to learn how to work as a team. Bernie had no choice, given the choices, and he withdrew his papers of retirement.

The *Point Banks* was in a shipyard the next morning. She was hauled from the water and stayed there for ten days as workers performed routine repairs. The workers also installed a "piggyback" gun mount on the bow. A .50-caliber machine gun and a trigger-fired 81-mm mortar were combined in one unit, and four .50-caliber machine gun mounts were installed aft. The little Boston Whaler, a 14-footer, was placed aboard.

By May 18, the cutter entered New York Harbor and moored at Staten Island. Bernie and the crew traveled into Manhattan to receive orders. They were to report to a base in California, they were told.

"We really haven't even had a chance to explain to our families what's going on here," Webber said. It wasn't right. They needed some time. He got them some, but not much. They could go to California via Boston. On the way, they had two days of liberty.

Then they flew out of Logan Airport for California and were gone. The cutter was hoisted onto a freighter and was shipped as deck cargo to the Philippines.

Less than a month after he had docked the *Point Banks* at Woods Hole, Bernie was headed to Vietnam. Never was he a pacifist, but never did he have making war in mind. The deployment was explained at first as search and rescue off the coast of Vietnam, but that quickly morphed into search and destroy. The 82-foot cutters drew only a few feet of water. They were worked with the Swift Boats in riverine warfare. They patrolled, lead raids, evacuated trapped units, and served as fire support.

"It was the coldest thing I've ever seen done," said one colleague of Bernie's at the time. "They took a man who had devoted his life to saving lives and asked him to take lives. He was in a lot of pain," the colleague said. "A lot of pain."

Webber remains silent about his service except to say that it was a depressed time in his life. There is a picture of him in his files that shows him in Da Nang in 1965. His notation says only, "Saving lives no longer of prime importance." He is carrying a carbine in the picture, but it is by no means a prop. Look closely at it and you can see the clip has an extra clip duct-taped to it so that rapid exchange is possible. It is a carbine rigged for combat, not show.

Bernie went over with his crew and spent about a year there. At home the war tore the country apart, and even in his blessed town of Chatham there were problems. Bernie had been the poster boy for the Coast Guard deploying to Vietnam. He was serving his country, his service, and, just as important, his crew. He was not trying to make a statement about politics or the war.

But at home, Miriam and his children became the center of attention for those who opposed and supported the war. They felt incredible pressure to bear up, and it did not help that Bernie was not there. In those emotional times, you were a baby killer if you supported the war, or a peacenik hippie if you opposed it. Finally, the Webber family moved off the Cape and down to Florida, to escape the local notoriety.

Bernie came back, spent a few months aboard a buoy tender, and retired on September 1, 1966, disillusioned and convinced the Coast Guard as he knew it had changed into something quite different. "The politics of the day divided traditional service philosophy," he wrote. "The values inbred in me over a twenty-one year period no longer seemed to apply or have any relation to the new image in the process of being developed by the service." He never elaborated much further, and has not to this day—except to say that the relationship between enlisted men and their officers was far closer when he first started out.

The CG 36500 was still whole at that time, but he knew she was headed for a burning on the beach. The vessel was a symbol of his own career.

It was not so much that he had left the Coast Guard, he implied, but that the Coast Guard had left him. Both he and the CG 36500 had outlived their usefulness as a symbol of the Coast Guard culture of courage.

As it turns out, he was wrong on both points.

Twenty-Six

BERNIE'S BOAT

May 2002
Chatham

His name was Webster, not Webber, and the year was 2000. Captain W. Russell Webster was in charge of the Coast Guard Group Woods Hole command on Cape Cod and Master Chief Boatswain Mate Jack Downey invited him to a "pinning" ceremony for new chief petty officers.

A chasm still existed between Coast Guard officers like Webster and non-commissioned officers like Downey and the petty officers. Webster and Downey thought they might close it and Webster was interested in the ceremony—a tradition that was local to the Cape.

The pinning ceremony involved mixing together the collar devices for new chief petty officers and seasoned chief petty officers. The intent was to underline traditions and symbolize the uninterrupted line of Coast Guard values and culture.

But one set of devices, worn smooth with time, was held aside and given to the newest chief petty officer. What's that about? Webster queried.

Those devices were worn by Bernie Webber, Downey said. They've been worn by nineteen new chief petty officers over the years. It lets the men know they are standing on the shoulders of heroes, Downey said.

That sent Webster to work researching the *Pendleton* rescue. It was a new era for the Coast Guard and Webster could not for the life of him understand how such a hero had been more or less shunned by the Coast Guard brass for nearly forty years. What he found was, in his words, "an unkind Coast Guard officer corps" that seemed to punish Webber for the sin of being too big a hero.

The enlisted men and the non-commissioned officers still held Webber in a reverent regard. He was a man who reflected the purest values of the culture and never knuckled under. And so the collar devices were passed through the decades, and would be for generations to come. It was almost as if an ancient oral tradition retold the story over the years, and in that manner the men in the ranks kept the memory of Webber alive.

The officers on the other hand had used Webber when they needed him, then threw him away. Or so it seemed to some.

Webster set out to correct that wrong. He had ascended to chief of operations of the First Coast Guard District headquartered in Boston by 2002—and in that position, he had some juice. His view was that the Coast Guard was on the right path these days, but needed to honor its heritage. He had researched the *Pendleton* rescue and contrasted it with the modern day world of search and rescue.

Modern craft, he noted in one article, are built with state-of-the-art composites and reinforced steel. Yet they will only go out in 30-foot seas. Webber's wooden craft challenged waves twice that high.

A modern crew wears three layers of especially designed clothing to protect them from the water and cold. Each rig costs about $2,000. Bernie and his crew wore old rubber pull-over boots, crude foul weather gear, and, Webster wrote, "mittens you would find appropriate for your kids when they went to school on a cold, dry day. "Today's

Guardsmen are appropriately given orders to employ risk-based decision models that optimize the chances of the crew coming back alive. Larger Coast Guard cutters, a 110-foot Island cutter for example, have 'survival' as a primary mission when seas are greater than 15 feet. Yesterday's lifesavers' motto was 'You have to go out, but you don't have to come back.'"

He wasn't saying the modern Coast Guard was wrong but that it could learn from the old Coasties. Learn from them and honor them as well.

Others had tackled another refurbishing job. The CG 36500 "retired" from service about two years after Bernie did. She was destined for a fire on the beach when someone spared her that fate. She was parked in the dunes instead, more or less abandoned for years.

The Orleans Historical Society learned that the famous boat was still around and set out to restore her. It was a huge undertaking. The wooden boat had deteriorated after being exposed to the elements for more than a decade. But with time, money, and patience, the society succeeded. They not only repaired the boat but made her operational—as good or better in the water than she was in 1968.

Bernie was aware of all this. He had been asked to help in the restoration. He did, but warily. He was tired of being used—by officers, by writers, by causes he could not verify. He vetted the historical society, found them to be good people, and was thrilled when the CG 36500 became waterborne and reborn in 1981. But so many folks over the years had tried to make a buck off him, he had little trust left.

So when Webster called him in 2001 and proposed that the crew reunite at Chatham in 2002 to commemorate the fiftieth anniversary of the rescue, Bernie Webber nearly hung up on him. Just another Coast Guard officer looking to score, was his original thought.

But Webster wasn't like that. It was a new Coast Guard, he told Bernie, and the men and women needed to know upon whose shoulders they stood. Webber could set any ground rules he wanted. The idea was to honor the crew and the boat. Nothing more.

Webber bit. He had not seen most of the crew of the CG 36500 in more than four decades, nearly five. Once the run was done back then, they more or less went their separate ways. If Webster was straight, if he was a man of honor, Webber thought, then it would be worth it.

But Webster needed to get all four crewmen together. All of them. If one could not come, then the deal was off.

Webster agreed to all the conditions and on a May afternoon in 2002, Webber, Maske, Livesey, and Fitzgerald walked down a pier in Chatham—and there she was. The CG 36500 rocked at pier side, as trim and shipshape as she was in 1952.

Bernie Webber and the crew are welcomed back to Chatham Coast Guard Station in May 2002.

The men fired up the engine and with Coast Guard personnel steering at first, veered again toward the Chatham Bar. The weather was calm, the bar was not threatening, the tide was right. The passage over the bar

At the fiftieth anniversary of the rescue: the crew of the CG 36500—Bernard Webber, Andrew Fitzgerald, Richard Livesey (deceased), and Irving Maske (deceased).

was as smooth as could be and the men and boat circled back to the pier and a ceremony. A Coast Guard helicopter flew over and flared off in salute. And then Webber asked all the officers and civilians to leave him alone with the enlisted men at Chatham station. It is not known what they talked about but they talked for quite a while. These were the men Bernie knew as real Coast Guard. These were his people.

Maske was the first of them to die on October 7, 2003. At Maske's funeral near Marinette, Wisconsin, a Coast Guard honor guard showed up, arranged by Captain Webster. No one at home really understood what Maske had done fifty years ago, but Webster did. The honor guard fired a gun salute. They gave his daughter, Anita, the flag from the coffin. Inside were three spent shells from the salute.

"The reason we are here is because we are taking your Dad's honor with us, so it will always be alive," a Coast Guardsman told her. The young man was crying as he said that, she noted.

Livesey died in 2008, in February, almost on the anniversary of the wreck. Bernie wrote a eulogy. He could still remember Livesey saying, "I'll go with you Webb."

Fitzgerald and Webber remain living legends to the Coast Guard enlisted men, and to the officers as well these days. Bernie was invited to speak at the Coast Guard Academy some time ago and is convinced there is a new Coast Guard out there that reveres the old values. He was proud of what the Coasties did during Hurricane Katrina.

The CG 36500 draws crowds on Cape Cod. The letters and numbers are the only official name she has ever had. But the people who know the legend often skip those formalities. In conversation, they do give her a name. "Oh, that's Bernie's boat," they will say. "That was Bernie's boat in the rescue."

Afterword

THIRD TANKER DOWN

A few of my more cynical friends in the newspaper business would occasionally joke, "Never let the facts get in the way of a good story." I always felt it worked the other way around, not because I stood on any grand ethical high ground but because I've found that if you gather some good facts and string them together they make a far better story than fantasy.

That's what I hope I've done here. I hope I've told a good story about some good people who did some good things. The fact that Bernie Webber, the hero here, ran into some bad times does not change the good that was done. It shows, I hope, that life is more complex for heroes than we might think, and it took Bernie Webber as much courage to lead a life of integrity and authenticity after the rescue as it did for him to shoot the Chatham Bar. Exposing the fact that life can be unfair isn't much of a story. Showing that one can live an honorable life nonetheless is, to my mind, a great story.

This story also shows, I hope, that over time what goes around comes around in a positive way. We do learn as a society, or at least we did here. Anyone can interpret an author's work as he or she will. I can say without qualification that my intent here is to bring a rough, real-world optimism to the reader. Life can be unfair. In its longer wave cycles, life can be fair as well.

So that is what I feel the facts have yielded here. But there is a funny thing about facts when one is writing narrative piece of non-fiction. In the researching, I don't think enough facts can be gathered. In the writing, I think facts need to be carefully, fairly, and sparely selected.

There is a difference, editor Gene Roberts taught me long ago, between an "at-length" report and an "in-depth" report. The former throws facts at an issue and hopes some stick. The latter marshals facts in a manner that is understandable by the reader, fair to its subject matter, and, one hopes, compelling.

So if you are telling a story in a narrative non-fiction form, as I am here, the selection and ordering of details become crucial. Often, the hardest part of writing a non-fiction narrative is deciding what to leave out. As a researcher, you can become committed to a story within a story because of the time it took in obtaining that fact. As a writer, you must be aware of meandering fact and know the difference between what is essential and fair to the story, and what is self-indulgent.

I know that well because I spent weeks researching the *Pendleton* and the *Fort Mercer* back in 2000. I fell in love with the story then and attempted to make it a part of my first maritime book, *Until the Sea Shall Free Them*. At the end of the day, a lengthy interlude about the wrecks of the *Pendleton* and *Fort Mercer* just did not work in a story about the wreck of the SS *Marine Electric*.

Here, I hope I've learned my lesson. I've attempted to keep this a short and seemingly simple narrative by avoiding too many "side trips." Still, I've learned that maritime readers can be exacting. Others may wonder of some passages, "How did he conclude that?"

So, I feel the "left out" parts are worth mentioning here to those readers with those questions and curiosities. Besides, I am, in some ways, revising a holy text of the Coast Guard here, and some of the facts need anchoring beyond mere source notes and secondary references.

The slowness of institutions to adapt new technology always fascinates me. So it was tempting to write at length about why the Coast Guard did not have helicopters on hand in 1952, when they were commonly in use in Korea at the time.

Details of the battle to adapt helicopters for search and rescue use within the Coast Guard can be found in *Wonderful Flying Machines: A History of U.S. Coast Guard Helicopters* by Barrett Thomas Beard (Annapolis, Maryland: Naval Institute Press, 1996). It's a well-researched volume about the conflict between too-well-meaning, very colorful Coast Guard officers and interesting enough that I had to simply walk away from the computer keyboard at times to keep from writing about it here.

It took even more effort to refrain from writing more background about the conversion of the 36-foot lifeboats to the 44-foot lifeboats and to elaborate on another earlier effort, in England, to improve rescue boats. The Royal Air Force was seeking faster rescue boats, ones that would stand up and plane in the water and reach downed pilots sooner. One of its main proponents was a simple airman named Shaw. If he had any disproportionate power at all, it is because his real name was T. E. Lawrence, or as he was famously known, Lawrence of Arabia. Lawrence was consumed by his command during World War I and sought solace and anonymity in the ranks. His efforts, along with many others, are credited with improving rescue boats that saved thousands during World War II. If you picture the PT boats of the American Navy during World War II, you'll have a good idea of the boats Lawrence helped develop.

Other parts of this book are most decidedly "left in" but deserve some elaboration as to why I wrote what I did or seemed to favor one interpretation over various others.

We'll start from the simplest here. Was the SS *Ohio* a T-2 tanker or a prototype? While this may seem like hair splitting to some, I have learned that many maritime readers can engage in skull splitting when a writer too glibly treats maritime terms or ship designations. (The experts out there who find error in my work or disagree with my conclusions are welcome to post them at www.twotankersdown.com.)

The *Ohio* is clearly listed as a T-2 in Andrew G. Spyrou's definitive, *From T-2 to Supertanker: Development of the Oil Tanker, 1940–2000* (Lincoln, Nebraska: iUniverse, 2006). Consequently, I identify the tanker as such in the text, even though I have some lingering doubts. The ship dimensions seem off to me for a T-2 and so does the time of construction. Regardless, the *Ohio* seems at the very least a good proxy for the T-2 and fitting to the example and context of the passage. She was welded—used the "dirty steel" of wartime suppliers—and she held up under vicious enemy attacks.

Other omissions and confusions worthy of discussion include exactly how the four men were lost from the bow section of the *Fort Mercer*. It is not that I found conflicting accounts of how the men were lost but rather they were vague accounts. The official report of the Marine Board of Investigation says simply that the *Yakutat* streamed down a line of rafts, and four men from the *Fort Mercer* bow jumped but didn't make it.

Normally, in such broad summaries, I found that I could dive into the actual testimony of the men involved and find more detail and nuance. But there just wasn't anyone who clearly viewed the jumps on the *Fort Mercer* side. The survivors there were exhausted, and the officers were forward searching for a lifejacket. They do not know why the men jumped.

Nor is the formal testimony of the *Yakutat* officers terribly helpful. They were hundreds of yards away and out of touch with the men, save through blinker and loudspeaker.

The version I present in the book is, I believe, the closest to what happened. It is based on comments made by Commander Naab after the formal marine boards. He told writers for *Colliers* magazine that the line of rafts strung together to rescue the men broke free and swerved toward them. The men on the cutter watched in horror as the men on the tanker bow jumped for the rafts far too soon, thinking this was their one chance.

Even then there seems to be a conflict or confusion of story. By testimony, three men jumped for the rafts and were lost. The fourth did not. The *Yakutat* came closer to the *Fort Mercer* bow—to relay verbal instructions, I believe—and that is when the fourth man jumped, thinking the *Yakutat* was offering rescue, as represented in the book. It seems to me the most accurate representation, but it does not mean I have it 100 percent right. Nor does it mean that I am either attempting to inject new controversy into the rescue or faulting Naab and the *Yakutat*'s performance.

Similarly, the rescue attempt of "Tiny Myers" took place in a swirl of activity, and there are differing accounts as to how he descended the ladder. The most widely circulated one is clearly false. The legend of the rescue was that Tiny himself was a super hero of the day, waiting at the bottom rung of the ladder and helping all of his shipmates into the CG 36500. As the last man down, he was tragically lost.

Myers was no more and no less a hero on a day of heroes, but the last-man-down story clearly is not true. Webber confirmed this in Theresa Mitchell Barbo, W. Russell Webster, and John Galluzo's *The* Pendleton *Disaster Off Cape Cod: The Greatest Small Boat Rescue in Coast Guard History* (Charleston, South Carolina: The History Press, 2007). It is also clear in the marine board testimony taken back in 1952. Cluff and Sybert, to make the family of Tiny Myers feel a little bit better about the mariner's death, cooked up the Tiny "public story."

In fact, there was nothing in Myer's behavior on board that would lead them not to feel proud of him. He played a crucial role in pulling on the whistle lanyard hour after hour and letting those on land know the *Pendleton* was in danger. The effort must have been tiring for a man who was out of shape and weighed well over 350 pounds.

The fact that he may have been outside for protracted periods of time led me to pursue a theory that I cannot prove, and so I did not want to put it in the body of the book. I do believe it is worth consideration, however: Myers may have been in a very advanced stage of hypothermia and would not have survived the rescue even had he made it to the boat.

It should be noted that Myers, when he descended the Jacobs ladder, was described as partially clad. Some accounts said he wore only a lifejacket; others that he was in his briefs.

There are many explanations for this, of course. Waves pounding him on the Jacobs ladder could have easily ripped off his pants. But it is also possible that Myers was in the throes of "paradoxical undressing," an advanced stage of hypothermia. If he had been outside for many hours pulling the lanyard on the whistle, he might well have been suffering from advanced hypothermia. In such a state, blood moves from the outermost extremities toward the heart to keep the basic functions going. The blood in the extremities is colder.

In advanced stages, the blood sometimes shifts from the central organs to the exterior extremities. When the warm blood rushes to the extremities, the hypothermic victim sometimes feels as if he is on fire. He is dying from the cold but paradoxically strips off his clothes because he feels so terribly hot. Death in such cases usually comes within thirty minutes if not treated, as the cold blood rushes to the heart and causes infarction.

No one in testimony described Myers stripping off his clothes. But no one knew what paradoxical undressing was at the time. And everyone was sensitive to Myer's memory. What might have happened here is that Myers stripped off his own clothes while in advanced hypothermia and was very close to death when he attempted to descend the ladder. If that theory is true, then he almost certainly would not have made it back alive, even if he had landed in the boat. It also would deepen the irony of the CG 36500 crew, who suffered for many years from guilt attached to Tiny's death.

It's an interesting theory and one I believe quite plausible, but in the end I did not feel I had enough confirming facts to include it.

Webber and the crew, even on the fiftieth anniversary of the rescue, said as if one that they thought every day of their lives about the loss of Tiny Myers. In today's world, we would no doubt diagnose this as survivor's guilt or as a form of post-traumatic stress disorder. Webber himself in one book allowed as how the Coast Guard in his day did not have the counseling services of the modern Coast Guard, and he suggested that counseling is a good thing.

My hope is that Webber has found ease from that burden over the years, but I did not want to deconstruct and seem to minimalize a 1950s event in terms of twenty-first century psychological knowledge. The pain they carried cannot be dismissed as needless. It was the hero's burden. That such a burden can be made lighter today thanks to counseling insights is good. But it does not lesson the pain they carried. Psychobabble can easily creep into stories, and I didn't want that to happen here. Never mistake the fact that the men and women we send out into such situations, whether rescue work or war, will encounter these burdens.

The rescue at the *Pendleton* stern is told from a number of different viewpoints. Not all of them agree totally, but none of them seem contradictory either. Men were landing in the boat, near the boat, bouncing onto and off the boat. It seems only logical that a bit of chaos might ensue. So my sources here are from Webber, from testimony from the crew of the *Pendleton*, and from other accounts from the CG 36500 crew. All of them agree in one important way: all that could be done to rescue Tiny Myers was done. Everyone worked together—the rescuers and the rescued.

One new fact my story makes public is that Sybert was not the last man down the ladder, as Webber thought true and stated in *The* Pendleton *Disaster*. The testimony shows clearly that Sybert descended earlier. Again, this is not intended as any criticism of Sybert, who seemed to have deserved a medal of his own from all that I could see.

A longer theme contained within this story may be not readily apparent, but here it is: the enlisted men and the officers of the Coast Guard went through a prolonged period of "cultural drift" in the last part of the twentieth century. While it is touched on here, I would urge you to read just about anything written by Dennis Noble on the matter. He is a Coastie-turned-historian, and he brings an important perspective to bear. The fact that Webster, an officer, showed such respect for enlisted men is, I hope, indicative of how the gap between the ranks is closing.

Of last note is the context of how the wrecks of the *Pendleton* and *Fort Mercer* fit into another piece of Coast Guard history. It is a history that saw not only its own tragedy, but also an eventual turnaround. The story of *Until the Sea Shall Free Them* does not fit inside *Two Tankers Down* any more than *Two Tankers Down* fits inside *Until the Sea Shall Free Them*.

Still, the *Pendleton* and the *Fort Mercer* marked an important time in Coast Guard inspection history, and the readers of this book should benefit a bit from the context of that history.

One has to ask what lessons were learned from the fact that two identical tankers known to contain flaws split in two at exactly the same time? Did the merchant mariners, the Coast Guard, and the shipowners change the acceptable level where risk and reward balanced out?

Not appreciably.

There were commendations for the brave crew and officers of the Coast Guard and of the merchant vessels. Captain Russell Webster has noted how exceptional this was. "In all, 24 Coast Guardsmen were honored for their efforts during the *Fort Mercer–Pendelton* rescues," he wrote. "Seventy of the possible 84 crewmen were eventually saved from the broken vessels. Five Gold Lifesaving Medals, four Silver Lifesaving Medals, and 15 Coast Guard Commendation Ribbons were awarded to the rescuers.

"On average, five Gold Lifesaving Medals and 10–12 Silver Lifesaving Medals are awarded each year for acts of heroism on the water."

But in some ways the heroism upstaged the more insidious matters of inspection and seaworthiness. The Coast Guard Marine Board of Inquiry blamed the sinkings on structural failure, complicated by load distribution and the storm. But at the heart of it was the structural inadequacy of all ships built prior to 1948, when new steel standards were used.

The board conceded that the crack arrestors thought to stop this sort of damage really didn't, and the boards of the *Fort Mercer* and *Pendleton* were saying the crack arrestors really weren't intended to actually stop structural failure. They were just designed to keep the ships afloat long enough to reach harbor or aid.

As the report on the *Fort Mercer* stated, "It was felt at the time that the measure proposed would provide the means of preventing complete failure of the hull, and, that while fractures could still be expected to occur under some circumstances, the ships would be able to get into port."

But, the Coast Guard said, additional measures would be taken after the crack-ups off Cape Cod. T-2 tankers would be fitted with four more crack arrestors, and the bilge keep attachment would be riveted, not welded. New loading manuals would be issued, and the longitudinal strength of the ship would be fortified.

"This, together with research programs to determine the fundamental causes of fractures of ships, should enable us to achieve the standards of safety desired on American ships."

Those words kept the T-2s at sea.

Later, mariners would find that not even twelve crack arrestors could stop the structural failures.

Everyone recognized the heroism of the 1952 rescues, and rightfully so, but no one adequately recognized the underlying causes of the catastrophe that put the rescuers and the rescued at risk. The shortsightedness in 1952, shared by all maritime institutions and the press, was more astounding because the *Pendleton* and *Fort Mercer* weren't the only old ships falling apart at the time.

Another victim of the old steel was the SS *Pennsylvania*. Had the appropriate lessons from the *Pennsylvania* been learned, the *Pendleton* and *Fort Mercer* might not have sailed to their catastrophes.

The next to last voyage of the SS *Pennsylvania* found her departing Long Beach in November 1951, bound for Yokohama. Fifteen hundred miles out she was swept by a severe storm. On November 6, the main deck plating of the converted liberty ship cracked to the right of the main house on the ship. She turned 180 degrees and headed home to Portland. The fracture ought to have been a warning. It was not. Repairs were made. Risks would be taken. The ship was re-certified. Then it was dry-docked and everything found up to snuff. If the crew, officers, Coast Guard, or shipyard managers were forewarned by the fracture of the main deck, they did not express it.

So on paper, the seven-year-old ship was fit and trim. On January 2, 1952, no doubt with the optimism brought by a new year, the *Pennsylvania* put her fractured main deck behind her and loaded wheat and barley in Vancouver. Eighteen "Army type" trailers were stowed on her deck, and two Army dump trucks—about sixty-eight tons of deck cargo in all—lashed to with No. 9 wire. She rounded Port Angeles, Washington, and discharged her pilot on January 5.

But four days later the ship ran into gale-force winds. Waves of 35 to 40 feet pounded the vessel. At around 7:00 a.m., George Plover, the master, radioed that the *Pennsylvania* had sustained yet another fracture. The deck was fine. This time the fracture was in the hull. It ran from the sheer strake (the top of the hull) to the engine room. The ship was turning and would try to make Seattle, Plover said.

Frantic dispatches followed as the ship struggled for its life. The vessel could not be steered—a profound problem in 40-foot seas. The vessel was taking on water in the engine room and the number one hold. She would need assistance.

The crew and officers struggled to repair the steering. Then the deck load came adrift, more than sixty tons of skittering trucks. This ripped the tarps from the forward hatches. The crew could not go forward because of the pandemonium caused by the waves and loose eighteen-ton trailers. This meant, in all probability, that the ship was taking in more water in the holds through the less-secure hatches.

Then Plover radioed that the steering gear was fixed. That was the good news. The bad news was that the vessel was so down by the head—listing so far forward—that the rudder was tilted out of the water too much to allow steering.

Now number two hatch was filled with water as well, as the gale continued to pound the ship. Plover said his only hope was for the weather to moderate. It did not, and the last dispatch, at eleven minutes before midnight on January 9, 1952, said the crew and officers were abandoning ship.

One lifeboat was later found in the area. Nothing else—ever. No debris. No life rings. No logs or journals. The *Pennsylvania* was simply gone.

A greater mystery followed. The U.S. Coast Guard conducted a Marine Board of Investigation on the disappearance of the SS *Pennsylvania*. Not surprisingly, the board concluded "this casualty was the result of a structural failure due, at least in part, to unusual stresses created by gale-force winds and heavy seas."

Then the board added, "Since so little is known of the origin and extent of this structural failure, the Board is unable to submit recommendations for prevention of future casualties of this nature. The Board recommends that no further action be taken and that this case be closed."

While the statement was literally true—the board did not know exactly what caused the fracture and what sort of fracture it was—it was disingenuous at best in the context of World War II welded vessels. The history of brittle fractures among pre-1948 ships was well established and, lacking other evidence to the contrary, it would be logical to conclude that this was another instance. Or at least that there was a high probability requiring a lot of action.

Perhaps even more bizarre was the commandant's review. He disagreed that the 14-foot hull fracture letting water into the holds and engine room was the primary cause of the sinking. "It would appear that the heavy weather encountered with consequent coming adrift of the deck cargo, flooding of numbers one and two holds, steering gear failure, and inability to manage the vessel in the heavy sea contributed to a greater extent to the foundering of the *Pennsylvania* than did the structural failure."

This struck some observers as strange. If the *Pennsylvania* had been a swimmer, would the commandant had concluded that it was not the bullet through the lungs that caused the victim's death but the failure of his arms and legs to function properly that kept him from swimming?

The commandant repeated a mantra regarding the condition of the steel.

"In connection with the structural failures, the susceptibility of welded ships to extensive fractures has been known and a serious problem since early in World War II, when our shipyards turned to welding as the only means of fulfilling the task set before them of rapidly building enough ships to support the war effort . . . A great deal has been learned since 1943 when the *Schenectady* broke in two. . . ."

"These lessons resulted, among other things, in the fitting of 'crack arrestors,' belts of steel riveted into the old Liberty ships and the T-2 tankers and the C-4 troopships," he noted. "Ships built since 1948, with higher standards of steel, are not experiencing these brittle fracture problems," he said. And the Coast Guard must continue to keep a close eye on the old vessels, but continued research, crack arrestors, and inspections "should enable us to achieve the standards of safety desired on American ships."

Those words of optimism might have been more comforting had they not been written on July 16, 1952, nearly six months *after* two wartime T-2 tankers, the *Pendleton* and the *Fort Mercer*, ran into trouble on the same day in the same storm in the same general location off Cape Cod.

It seems to me that in this context of consistent catastrophic failure and loss of life that the Coast Guard, the regulators, the Congress, the press, the maritime unions, and the crewmen and officers themselves were far more interested in how to justify keeping the ships afloat than inquiring into the safety of the ships. On one level, it is wholly understandable. The American maritime sector was shrinking. Jobs were hard to come by.

On another level, at least five hundred lives were lost on old ships that sailed with defective steel—or were far past their "shelf date."

By 1963, when the Marine *Sulphur Queen* disappeared, there were eighteen cases of T-2 structural failures over the years.

Then in March 1964, the modified T-2 tanker, the SS *San Jacinto*, suffered an explosion and cleanly split in two off the eastern shore of Virginia. The bow bobbed off and the stern managed just fine, thanks.

Scrub down the paint on the *San Jacinto* and one might just have found the faint lettering, "Fort Mercer." The stern of the *Fort Mercer* had been salvaged and fitted to a new bow. The *Fort Mercer* had, in effect, sunk twice. Or at least her bow had.

The *San Jacinto* was, for all intents and purposes—twelve years after the sinking of the *Fort Mercer* and the *Pendleton*—the third tanker down. The *Fort Mercer* stern had survived two catastrophes and lost two bows.

Only decades later, in 1985, did another Coast Guard hero, Captain Domenic A. Calicchio, halt the use of the old ships through an impassioned effort as a member of the Marine Board of Investigation that examined the wreck of the *Marine Electric*. Calicchio, I had sought to show in my first book, shot the bureaucratic equivalent of the Chatham Bar. In doing so, he lost his career but rescued the system from an errant path.

Both Calicchio's bureaucratic heroism and Bernie Webber's nautical heroism sprang from the same traditions and a culture of courage. The new Coast Guard does indeed now honor both men appropriately as heroes, and it is cheering that such matters are turned right in the cycles of time. It is also sobering to think they could again turn wrong.

The Gold Medal Crew steers the CG 36500 again toward Chatham Bar, more than fifty years after the rescue, in May 2002 (author's photo).

Acknowledgments

Bernard C. Webber was patient and gracious enough to answer dozens of questions in the course of my researching and writing this book. He also allowed me to draw heavily upon his autobiographical accounts published in his book, *Chatham, "The Lifeboatmen."* That said, it should be clear that this is not an official biography, and it does not speak for Mr. Webber.

Captain Robert M. Cusick and Captain Fred Calicchio were equally gracious to read my first drafts of this piece and correct my improper usage of nautical terms. Richard Hiscock was invaluable in checking Coast Guard terminology, Chatham geography, and the rescue in general. All of them kept me from using "ropes" when I meant "lines."

Candace Clifford of Cypress Communications provided critical archival research. I would recommend her services highly to anyone interested in penetrating the stored records of Coast Guard investigations (www.lighthousehistory.info).

Tom McCarthy, Cynthia Hughes, Ellen Urban, and Christine Duffy at Lyons Press were indefatigable in supporting this book and seeing it through from conception to print.

Sterling Lord and Robert Guinsler, my literary agents, were supportive and encouraging over the years.

I am also grateful to the authors whose works are cited here. Their previous work enabled me to understand the rescues and build a bit more upon the body of knowledge. Any mistakes of fact or interpretation contained in the book are mine and mine alone, however. I would encourage readers who believe they have found mistakes to post them at www.twotankersdown.com.

For those moved by the events concerning the CG 36500, please look over the foundation Web page at www.cg36500.org for more information about supporting the effort to keep her story alive.

Source Notes

Note: In the original draft, I had included approximately two hundred footnotes. To avoid risking a narrative that was too academic in nature, my editors and I decided to omit footnotes in the text and provide endnotes as fashioned here. So, below you will find noted passages in the book followed by their general sources. Most times, I sourced a passage because it may be new to the lore of the 1952 rescues, or a reader might plausibly ask, "Where did he come up with that?" Those who have questions about sources or corrections should post them to www.twotankersdown.com.

—Robert Frump

CHAPTER ONE

The big tanker, nearly the size of two football fields, stretched end-to-end, lay at dockside, half-filled with 15,000 tons of heating oil and kerosene...
Marine Board of Investigation, February 1952, the SS *Pendleton*

Even Daniel Ludwig, now the multi-millionaire owner of fleets of tankers, found out what could happen back in 1926 when he was a young captain in Boston on the tanker Phoenix.
Jerry Shields, *The Invisible Billionaire Daniel Ludwig*
(Boston: Houghton Mifflin Company, 1986)

. . . a warm, summerlike night, February 12, 1952. . .

Weather Source, report for Baton Rouge, February 10–12, 1952,

www.weather-source.com (paid search)

This was a time when any tanker captain got the jitters.

Interview by the author with Captain Robert M. Cusick,

July 2000, Oldsboro, New Hampshire

Besides, there were stories, too, on how tough a ship those T-2s were. How about the SS Ohio?

Andrew G. Spyrou, *From T-2 to Supertanker: Development of the Oil*

***Tanker, 1940–2000* (Lincoln, Nebraska: iUniverse, 2006)**

How could you say it? Some of the ships weren't solid. But you didn't know which ones, really. The Coast Guard and the American Bureau of Shipping had acknowledged the problem and required that the ships be reinforced. On the decks of both ships, and below as well, ran thick steel belts, or "crack arrestors."

Marine Board of Investigation, testimony, March 1952,

the SS *Pendleton*, the SS *Fort Mercer*

There was a time and place he dreamed of little but surviving, after all: June 23, 1943, the tanker Stamvac Manilla, *in the southwest Pacific, not far from New Guinea.*

Marine Board of Investigation, testimony, March 1952, the SS *Fort Mercer*

CHAPTER TWO

Bernard C. Webber, a young lifeboat coxswain, had some slack time. He decided the new guys in command were growing on him, but he still missed dearly Frank Masachi and Alvin E. Newcomb, the old commander.

Masachi had saved Webber—but not physically, not literally as in a water rescue. If it had not been for Masachi and the discipline of the Coast Guard, Webber did not know where he would be. A kid in trouble was his guess.

Bernard C. Webber, *Chatham, "The Lifeboatmen:" A Narrative by a Seaman Recounting His Life in the Coast Guard at Chatham on the Southeast Corner of Cape Cod, Massach* (Orleans, Massachusetts: Lower Cape Publishing, 1985)

He made the case to his dad. Since age twelve, he'd been a Sea Scout, a water-going Boy Scout, with the Wollaston, Massachusetts troop. He loved the sea.

E-mail exchange, Bernard C. Webber and author, April 2008

Webber was on his way to the war. He joined his first ship in the Panama Canal, cocky as could be. He scrambled up a Jacobs ladder to the deck with a lit cigarette dangling from his mouth ready to take on the world.

E-mail exchange, Bernard C. Webber and author, April 2008

He strolled about and saw a large sign that said, "The Coast Guard Wants You." He was curious and popped into the office. There, a petty officer second class was eating lunch with his feet propped up on his desk. He took one look at young Webber and said, "What the hell do you want?"

Theresa Mitchell Barbo, W. Russell Webster, and John Galluzo, *The* Pendleton *Disaster Off Cape Cod: The Greatest Small Boat Rescue in Coast Guard History* (Charleston, South Carolina: The History Press, 2007)

"Hard jobs are routine in this service," read his letter of acceptance. "The Coast Guard is always at war; against all enemies of mankind at sea; fire, collision, lawlessness, gales, derelicts and many more."

E-mail exchange, Bernard C. Webber and author, April 2008

Bernie was among the first on the scene and recognized the body of Elroy Larkin. Nickerson was never found. It stunned Bernie. He knew the Chatham Bar could kill. But he had not seen firsthand the awesome strength of the ocean, the power of the waves on the bar to pitch-pole a 40-foot boat as if it were a tiddlywink flipped and spun by a thumb.

Webber, *Chatham*, "The Lifeboatmen"

It was Emro, the captain of the lightship, who finally intervened. A lieutenant was interrogating Masachi, and Emro could take it no more.

"Goddamn it! Who do you think you are?" he demanded of the officers from Boston.

Webber, *Chatham*, "The Lifeboatmen"

The Blue Book says we've got to go out," he snapped at the man. "It doesn't say a damn thing about having to come back."

David Wright and David Zoby, *Fire on the Beach: Recovering the Lost Story of Richard Etheridge and the Pea Island Lifesavers* (New York: Scribner, 2000)

CHAPTER THREE

Everyone thought bad welding was the problem. Everyone was pretty much wrong. Welding was visible and villainized but at best played a bit role. The problem, discovered only years later, lay not in something so obvious or visible, but at the molecular level. In 1954, tests would show conclusively that the steel used in the wartime ships contained too much sulfur and behaved badly in cold water.

Spyrou, *From T-2 to Supertanker*

She was handling nicely, Sybert thought, but early in the morning, before 5 a.m., a heavy sea washed over the poopdeck. It was nothing really, but notable enough to call to the bridge.

Marine Board of Investigation, testimony, March 1952, the SS *Pendleton*

Quickly, he found that one able-bodied seaman, Jacob Hicks, and another, Ray Steele, would take leadership positions. He came to think of Hicks as a makeshift chief mate, the ranking deck officer.

Marine Board of Investigation, testimony, March 1952, the SS *Pendleton*

He could maneuver the stern section a bit, but he knew they were drifting too rapidly toward shore—the Cape Cod shore where so many thousands of wrecks had washed up. If he attempted to steer and control too aggressively, the ship would pitch and lurch. There was little he could do other than go with the flow and steer to keep the stern section straight. He could not steam her farther out to sea, just keep her straight as she drifted. Every time he attempted to steer and maneuver, he could, briefly, but the forward exposed part of the stern dipped down and got drenched.

Marine Board of Investigation, testimony, March 1952, the SS *Pendleton*

Aaron Powell, a wiper, rigged up a line to the steam whistle. Another wiper was too small a man to work the rig himself; it took some heft to pull the line. So Powell drafted George "Tiny" Myers, an OS, ordinary seaman. He weighed more than three hundred pounds, not much of it muscle, it had to be said, but Tiny had plenty of spirit and enough weight to heave that whistle lanyard.

Marine Board of Investigation, testimony, March 1952, the SS *Pendleton*

CHAPTER FOUR

Nothing illustrated that better than the case of David Atkins, the heroic keeper of a Cape lifesaving station near Provincetown. In April 1879, a coal-carrying schooner, the Sarah J. Fort, *foundered a quarter mile off shore.*

Donna Hill, and David Atkins, *Hero of Cape Cod, Wreck and Rescue Journal*. "They Had to Go Out" collection of stories (Avery Color Studios, Inc., Gwinn, Michigan, 2007)

Two years earlier, he and some friends from the station had set out for Provincetown, at the tip of Cape Cod, to meet some P-town girls. The Provincetown scene was much wilder than Chatham, and Webber's intentions may not have been wholly honorable.

Webber, *Chatham, "The Lifeboatmen"*

The Pendleton's *crack-up began and ended in seconds. On the* Fort Mercer, *it began with a puzzle that solved itself only hours later.*

Marine Board of Investigation, testimony, March 1952, the SS *Fort Mercer*

Time it right and you might launch a boat in conditions like this one time out of a hundred. But then what for this small boat with no cover in waves far larger than the boat itself?

He'd lose at least half the crew, he figured. At least twenty men. Better for them to take their chances on the ship.

So he called the Coast Guard then and told them his position and that he needed assistance. No, he said, he could not say he was in dire straits. But he needed the Coast Guard to be ready in case he needed them.

Marine Board of Investigation, testimony, March 1952, the SS *Fort Mercer*

Not everyone on board the Fort Mercer *felt as comfortable with the crack arrestors as the captain. Not everyone, in fact, felt comfortable with the captain.*

186

Paetzel had ordered the men to be alert but had not sounded a general alarm. He did not want to sound any signals or bells that would stampede the crew. Word got out to some, but not to others. What followed was a combination of undue concern by some and unwarranted complacency among others.

Julio Molino, a seaman, was one of those who heard nothing from the master about the 8 a.m. crack. He did not have to be told. He was standing with a friend and looked out at sea.

Marine Board of Investigation, testimony, March 1952, the SS *Fort Mercer*

"Take the covers off the boats," he told Molino. And Molino did just that. He ran to the starboard lifeboat at the stern and cut the cover off the boat. Then he jumped in. The quartermaster moved to swing the boat out and lower it. The starboard side was taking the most wind.

"Calm down, calm down!" the bo'sun said. "Move to the port side."

Marine Board of Investigation, testimony, March 1952, the SS *Fort Mercer*

Word went down to Bushnell in the engine room and the chief engineer gently backed the engines astern. The smooth electro glide nature of the T-2 was still there; the half-ship responded and Bushnell maneuvered out of harm's way.

Marine Board of Investigation, testimony, March 1952, the SS *Fort Mercer*

On the stern, the men did not commemorate this historic event. They were excited, nearly a mob. They rushed the lifeboats. They were crowded around the starboard lifeboat, intent on piling in, lowering the boats and getting off the ship any way they could. The wind was blowing directly into them—the spray and snow and rain pelting them.

Laurence Whilley, an ordinary seaman, was there when a man from the mess (he did not know his name) yelled to Whilley above the howling weather: "Do you know how to pray?"

"Sure, I'm a Christian and a member of the church," Whilley yelled back. *"No one should be ashamed to pray."*

Marine Board of Investigation, testimony, March 1952, the SS *Fort Mercer*

A mild confrontation of sorts occurred then. C. W. Hindley was just the assistant cook, but he had been a combat marine and wanted to know what Bushnell thought. Hindley was disgusted at the lack of leadership and the panic at the boats. Never mind that Bushnell had been below, steering the stern out of the way of the bow. Bushnell was the senior officer. He should take charge. What was his assessment of the raft rescue, Hindley demanded.

Marine Board of Investigation, testimony, March 1952, the SS *Fort Mercer*

Then the Eastwind crew pulled on the lines and Ben Stabile, a gunnery officer on the Unimak, *thought the whole scene resembled the Cyclone ride at Coney Island. The raft was twisting up and down, torqued this way and that by the sea, blown about, turned nearly upside down, corkscrewed through the air.*

Charles B. Hathaway, *From Highland to Hammerhead: The Coast Guard and Cape Cod* (C. B. Hathaway, 2000)

One good thing was, they were all calm. They were nine men: the captain, the chief mate, the second mate, and the third mate. They were Jack Brewer, Fahrner, and Vince Guilden, respectively. Ed Turner, the purser who paid the bills and was essentially an accountant, was there, as was John V. Reilly, the radioman; they knew he was a good man to have on the blinker lights. Then there was the quartermaster, Culver, and the two seamen who had just joined the bridge five minutes before the ship split. Perley W. Newman was an experienced able-bodied seaman; Jerome C. Higgins was a young kid, an ordinary seaman.

Marine Board of Investigation, testimony, March 1952, the SS *Fort Mercer*

CHAPTER SIX

Cluff was the new guy and for the old guard Coasties like Masachi, he was too new and abandoned all traditions. Newcomb, the old commander, had a family in Chatham, but he did the same ten days on, two days off that his men did. His children would gather after school at the entrance to the Coast Guard station, hoping to catch a glimpse of their dad. But their dad would not go out to meet them. For the ten days on, his kids were all the Coasties inside the building.

Webber, *Chatham*, "The Lifeboatmen"

It was not unknown for men to be rescued from the bows of splintered tankers. This was what Eugene Ericksen had witnessed five years earlier on the SS Sacketts Harbor, *a T-2 cruising peacefully en route to Alaska in a cold but calm sea in 1947.*

He was on watch near the stern at around 1 a.m., embroidering the war stories he told now in peacetime, when he heard a thunderous crack and felt the ship rise up gently as if she had nosed over a speed bump. All the lights went out.

"We've hit something," he thought, but knew that was improbable and began running toward the bow of the ship.

Eugene Ericksen, telephone interview with the author, 2002

None of them stayed for below for long, though. Most of them instinctively crowded toward the top of the ship, and there, in a passageway that was sheltered, passed the time, exchanging stories, speculating on where the rescuers were, listening to the repeated danger signals that Tiny Myers blew, hour after hour.

Much of the talk was about launching the boats—and how impossible that seemed. Much of the talk, too, was what happened if the ship ran aground.

Marine Board of Investigation, testimony, March 1952, the SS *Pendleton*.

Just then, a great curl of water rose from behind the Pendleton *bow and swept through the bridge and over the deck. It came from behind the man after covering the bridge. The man on the rail was caught up from behind by the wave and was carried forward by it.*

He held on. He was on the outside of the ship now—on the wrong, ocean side of the rail—but he held on a long time. Then he seemed no longer able to keep his grip. And as his grip lessened, he leapt with all his might out from the ship, toward Bangs and the rescuers.

Marine Board of Investigation, testimony, March 1952, the
SS *Pendleton*

CHAPTER NINE

A strange procession of vehicles crawled out from Chatham toward Nauset Inlet. A DUKW and a Dodge four-wheel drive "power wagon" moved over the slippery beaches, buffeted by spray and wind.

Webber, *Chatham*, "The Lifeboatmen"

Cluff was silent for minutes. And then Cluff—knowing he was almost certainly pronouncing a death sentence for the young man—said slowly in his Virginia accent, "Webber, pick yourself a crew. Ya-all got to take the 36500 out over the bar and assist that thar ship, ya-heah?"

Webber heard all right, and a sinking feeling came to his stomach. No chance at the Chatham Bar. No chance! And why me? Why me? My wife is sick. I haven't spoken to her in two days. Why me? Instead, Webber said, "Yes sir, Mr. Cluff, I'll get ready."

Bernie Webber knew exactly who he wanted for the crew: all men he had worked with before. The only problem was, none of them were there. There wasn't even a full crew left in the station. Just a junior engineer, one seaman, and a guy from a lightship who was in transit, waiting for the storm to break to go out to his ship. He wasn't even a rescue guy. That was another reason not to go, another reason the mission was impossible. He could tell Cluff that.

Webber, *Chatham*, "The Lifeboatmen"

He had this odd habit, a humble one, forget about the jokes and stuff. Whenever they finished a patrol when Livesey was on board, no matter how trivial or routine, Livesey would have a single parting phrase to Bernie. "Thanks, Webb," he would say quietly. And there was no hint of a joke in it, no irony. Livesey was a good man. He got excited and enthusiastic, even if they were running supplies to a lighthouse.

Bernard C. Webber, eulogy for Livesey (sent to author), March 2008

"You guys going out in this?" Stello looked worried. Webber nodded grimly. "You guys better get . . . lost . . . before you get too far out," Stello said. In other words, say you gave it a try, then come back.

This was about as official a cultural permission to play it safe as Bernie could get. The roughest toughest fisherman in a tough fishing community was telling him to take a dive, to hit the mattress and stay down. There would be no goading slurs if Bernie did that.

"Call Miriam," Webber bellowed back.

Webber, *Chatham*, "The Lifeboatmen"

Then he thought: Who am I? What's my job? The question came to him in a calm way and the answer came in the same manner with great clarity. I am a Coast Guard first class boatswain mate . . . My job is the sea and to save those in peril upon it.

Webber, *Chatham*, "The Lifeboatmen"

CHAPTER TEN

In the chart room of the bow section of the Fort Mercer, *the general alarm—a Klaxon-like siren—continued to sound, powered by the emergency batteries on board the bow. None of the men seemed to notice the annoying noise. It was just a part of the chaos. Then Fahrner, the second officer, snapped the alarm switch off. The general alarm was loud enough to let men on board the ship know there was a problem, but not loud enough to serve as any sort of "rescue-us" signal to searchers.*

Marine Board of Investigation, testimony, March 1952, the
SS *Fort Mercer*

And so the men descended from the bridge to the main deck level. Paetzel and the radioman were the last two left. Paetzel was big, with a comfortable layer of fat to keep him warm. Sparks was very thin with no insulation from the cold. Still it was hard to tell who was shivering the hardest.
"Captain I'm not going to make it," Sparks said to Paetzel.
"You'll make it!" Paetzel replied. "Hold on until you reach the catwalk."

Marine Board of Investigation, testimony, March 1952, the
SS *Fort Mercer*

Aboard the Yakutat, *Naab watched with utter dread. They had been positioning the rafts to drift alongside the bow section, to get the rafts in close. This was easier said than done. The winds, the waves, the snow and rain all made it difficult to maneuver and drift the line down in the dark.*

And at precisely the wrong moment, the line to the rafts gave way. Just parted and let the rescue processional loose into the storm.

The rafts swooped sharply toward the bow section. Naab did not even have time to warn the seamen.

Fuller and Friedenberg, "The Coast Guard's Finest Hour," *Collier's*
(December 27, 1952)

Higgins interpreted it as another rescue effort. The cutter seemed convincingly close. He jumped the rail and leapt for the cutter, falling into the chaos of ocean between the ship and the half-ship. He was gone in ten seconds. No one had a chance to reach him. The sea just took him and there was no sight of his orange life jacket after one cycle of waves.

Marine Board of Investigation, testimony, March 1952, the
SS *Fort Mercer*

The cutter turned-to and left the Fort Mercer. *It was well past midnight and there seemed little she could do. The storm was not slackening. The flares from the plane comprised mood lighting for a horror scene, not visibility for a rescue. The survivors would have to hang on until daylight. Further rescues would lead to more harm now. They had to wait for better conditions. Naab felt the worse hour of his life as he realized this, then snapped back to command. There is nothing more we can do now, he thought. We need to just wait until daylight. His own crew had taken a beating in these seas. Everyone was exhausted and they needed some rest. Naab prayed that the old hulk would still be floating.*

Collier's

CHAPTER ELEVEN

Webber held on with all his might, trying, trying to steer the boat's bow to meet the next wave. The keel, the ton of bronze, was righting them, righting them, bringing them back. He was gunning the engine, powering the boat's bow to the next wave, jamming the throttle, working the gears, while still strapped to the wheel.

Webber, *Chatham*, "*The Lifeboatmen*"

CHAPTER TWELVE

And so it was that Sybert calculated what he would do. He could steer, some. If he put it full ahead, he could control the direction of the ship a bit. Move it away from the landside and a bit out to sea.

But each time he did that the exposed "bow" of the half-ship bucked and strained and the ship would pitch and yaw. It seemed to be taking on water. The lower engine room seemed to be filling with it. How watertight would his tanks stay?

It's inevitable, he thought. At some point, we're going to have to go aground.

Marine Board of Investigation, testimony, March 1952, the SS *Pendleton*

"Stop!" Sybert said. "We had better go on the beach than capsize."

And so he put the ship aground then: stopped the maneuvering of the engines and let the ship drift in on the bar. She touched the sand sweetly with only a bit of rock and sway.

Marine Board of Investigation, testimony, March 1952, the SS *Pendleton*

CHAPTER THIRTEEN

Warily, Bernie maneuvered the CG 36500. He moved along the port side of the hulk. There were no signs of life. Up above, steel railings were bent like pipe cleaners. All this way they had come, and no one was left alive, Webber thought. His heart sank at the uselessness of their effort.

Barbo, Webster, and Galluzzo, *The* Pendleton *Disaster*

Normally, the departure would be in terms of seniority, with the lowest rank going first and the officers staying behind. But this was a perilous venture—not an easy trip down a flight of stairs, but an unknown descent into fierce seas.

So Steele, it was decided, would go first. The able-bodied seaman was just that—as fit as anyone there. He would chart the way down.

Over he went. He did not like the top of the ladder. It seemed rotten both in rope and wood. But he did not tarry at the top. Down he went, with 4- to 5-foot gaps between the wooden plank steps. You had to have some upper body strength to do this. Hold on as you reached down with your foot almost an entire body length to the next plank. Slide down a bit with your hands, feet dangling for purchase on the next rung.

—**Marine Board of Investigation, testimony, March 1952, the SS** *Pendleton*

Harnessed still to the wheel, the young coxswain needed three hands to run the CG 36500: one for the wheel, one for the throttle and speed, one for the direction and gear shift of the boat. He was in constant motion and the shifting, the turning, none of it was on automatic power. Each shift, turn, and gear change took real physical effort.

Barbo, Webster, and Galluzzo, *The* **Pendleton** *Disaster*

Six men were left on top when Aaron Ponsel and Tiny Myers were next down the ladder. All night, they had been blowing the whistle. Now it was time to leave.

Marine Board of Investigation, testimony, March 1952, the
SS *Pendleton*

Waves slammed against him and it seemed as if he had lost his pants up there. The ladder would bow out with the sway of the half-ship, and then slam Tiny hard back against the steel hull. Webber thought he could hear the big man groan. It was a bizarre scene, this huge man, nearly naked, struggling down the ladder.

Webber, *Chatham,* **"The Lifeboatmen"**

And then Myers came to the bottom rung of the ladder, the last rung. The one that was a double length away from the next one up because a rung was missing. Strength seemed to go out of the big man then, and he hit the last rung with his feet and then with his knees. He was kneeling on the last rung, but it all looked lined up. The boat was there. "Jump!" someone yelled. It was unclear whether Tiny jumped or slipped.

Marine Board of Investigation, testimony, March 1952, the SS *Pendleton*

The crew caught Tiny with their spotlight. They could still see him. He was floating. They were perilously close to the ship's hull. Men were still coming down and landing on the boat, landing in the water. Tiny drifted toward the propeller of the ship. Webber could see him; he was still alive and their eyes locked. It was a look from Tiny, Webber thought, that said, "It's okay. It's okay."

Barbo, Webster, and Galluzzo, *The* Pendleton *Disaster*

David A. Brown, the first assistant engineer, was the last man down the ladder.

Marine Board of Investigation, testimony, March 1952, the SS *Pendleton*

CHAPTER FOURTEEN

So they told him then and there: you go first. Paetzel said no. Then we'll throw you over first, the two junior officers told him. Your choice.

Marine Board of Investigation, testimony, March 1952, the SS *Fort Mercer*

They had thought to bring the boat up on davits, but it was nearly sinking at shipside, so they brought the men up by cargo nets. Then, the little boat was lifted up as well. All the time, Kiley protested. He could make another run, he told Naab. He could do it again. One more time, Kiley said. He was sobbing now. Naab and the others thought it a miracle Kiley had even made it back at all. They would not let him go out again.

Collier's

Such a simple thing. Just open a pocket knife, a large pocket knife. Fahrner had the knife in his hands. He was commanding his fingers to grasp the blade, hold it against his thumb and just apply the half pound of pressure needed to open the blade.

His fingers did not respond. He could not feel them. He could not make them move. They might as well be stumpy pegs of half-frozen meat. In fact, they were.

Marine Board of Investigation, testimony, March 1952, the SS *Fort Mercer*

Wilfred Bleakley, a young ensign on the bridge of the Yakutat *just eight months out of the Coast Guard Academy, could stand it no longer. "You have no choice, Captain!" he bleated out. "Back down and hope the line breaks on the other side of the raft."*

Hathaway, *From Highland to Hammerhead*

CHAPTER FIFTEEN

He reached to the radio and then simply flipped it off.

Webber, *Chatham*, "The Lifeboatmen"

Webber did not try to be polite. He called the watchtower and said essentially that the only help he needed was when they got back to the fish pier. Perhaps someone could be there to help the survivors. Then he snapped the radio off again.

E-mail exchange between Bernard C. Webber and author, March 2008

CHAPTER SIXTEEN

At that exact moment, someone yelled, "There she goes!"

The survivors, still in the raft, looked over at the bow section. The half-ship turned over and sank the bow deck beneath the waves. Then the survivors swiveled their frozen necks and looked up at the Coast Guard. Ensign Bleakley would never forget the look on their faces—a combination of wonder, gratefulness, exhaustion, and amazement.

Hathaway, *From Highland to Hammerhead*

CHAPTER SEVENTEEN

Photographer Dick Kelsey was local to Cape Cod. He watched the big city newspaper boys carefully as they jockeyed for position. All of them were lined up at the Chatham Fish Pier as if it were the 50-yard line of the Rose Bowl. Like Kelsey, they held in their hands the big, cumbersome Speed Graphic cameras of the day, the type that used huge #2 flash bulbs and film holders.

Webber, *Chatham*, "The Lifeboatmen"

The seamen were near giddy. Some of them were exhausted and giddy, and one-by-one they began fainting: first one, then the other; sixteen in all. They were laughing one moment, then their eyes turned back and they floated to the floor. The town doctor, Dr. Carroll Keene, treated them all. They all recovered. The Rev. Steve Smith tended those who needed spiritual help or prayer.

Barbo, Webster, and Galluzzo, *The* Pendleton *Disaster*

CHAPTER EIGHTEEN

"For God's sakes, man, sink her!" said the officer on the salvage tug. "I'll take the responsibility myself."

Marine Board of Investigation, testimony, March 1952, the SS *Fort Mercer*

Frustrated, Commander Frank M. McCabe told the crew to ready depth charges. McCabe had served during the war on anti-submarine patrol and knew what underwater explosions could do to the buoyancy of sealed metal spaces. A depth charge essentially was a barrel full of high explosives rigged to go off underwater.

McCabe would fire the depth charges using a K-gun that hurled the barrels away from the cutter. He gave the order to pass the bow section at full speed so the cutter itself would not be harmed by the blast.

Hathaway, *From Highland to Hammerhead*

CHAPTER NINETEEN

"We killed a man back there." The thought struck Bernie even before he and the CG 36500 had reached homeport. The rest of the crew felt some variation of this.

Barbo, Webster, and Galluzzo, *The* Pendleton *Disaster*

What do you think of that?"

Bernie did not have to think about it at all.

"I think it stinks," he shot back to the officer. "For whatever reasoning it was determined I should receive the gold the same should apply to them. They were there; the risks were the same."

E-mail exchange between Bernard C. Webber and author, April 2008

Bangs essentially ran the station. And Bangs still felt immense guilt about not rescuing the man from the Pendleton *bow. Others began interpreting any action of Bernie's as putting on airs. Still others thought wrongly that he was making money from the rescue from all the speeches he made and all the articles that were written about him.*

Webber, ***Chatham,*** **"The Lifeboatmen"**

But Cluff and Sybert, the chief engineer of the Pendleton, *had cooked up a seemingly harmless story, what seemed at the time like a benevolent lie. They told the press and Myers's family that Tiny had been the last man down, that Tiny had been a hero himself standing on the last rung hoisting people into the boat with no regard to his own safety.*

Barbo, Webster, and Galluzzo, ***The*** **Pendleton** ***Disaster***

Again, Webber was handicapped in giving a clear answer to this because of exaggerations by Cluff of the radar's helpfulness. Radar was expensive, and Cluff wanted more of it. He spread the word that the radar had been of great help and the well-meant sophistry crept into the folklore of the rescue. Radar became a hero in the rescue as well.

In fact, no one, including Cluff, stated in the formal Marine Board of Investigation that radar helped Webber at any time. It was sketchy technology back then. The specialist at the screen was there to repair the radar, not run it. It did seem as if the radar helped locate the Pendleton, *which was an important feat. But it was far from a star that day.*

E-mail exchange between Bernard C. Webber and author, March 2008

Bernie was cast out. Or cast himself out. He transferred out to Masachi thinking that would end it. He was with his mentor now, on board the CG 833888 out of Woods Hole, second officer in command.

But even then the problems followed. He would be on duty, then get a call from the brass. He was needed at a speech here, an interview there.

Webber, *Chatham*, "The Lifeboatmen"

CHAPTER TWENTY-ONE

Bernie found that useful himself at times. How was he to explain the CG 36500? In his mind, the CG 36500 had done all the work. He was not hallucinating this. His hand had been off the wheel. The little boat with no navigating hand took them first to the wreck, then to the bait bucket, and then to Joe.

Was it spooky? Religious? Webber wasn't sure. That was between Joe, the boat, and God, as far as he was concerned.

Webber, *Chatham*, "The Lifeboatmen"

CHAPTER TWENTY-TWO

He had to say it. Nothing much bothered this boat. Would the Coast Guard be better off with the 36-footers or the new 44s? He had to go with the 44-footers and told the brass that. It was not what he wanted to say but what he had to say, because it was true.

Webber, *Chatham*, "The Lifeboatmen"

CHAPTER TWENTY-THREE

The Coasties were running by then. The men from Bernie's crew, Davidson and Chapius, immediately ran down the beach. It was as if they were in the old Etheridge days now. They had tried boats, and that had failed. They had tried the gun, and that had failed. There was nothing now to do but swim for him. Complete old school.

Webber, *Chatham*, "The Lifeboatmen"

CHAPTER TWENTY-FOUR

The lieutenant smiled back at him with what he thought was good news.

"Well, you fellows are going to Vietnam."

"You've got to be kidding," Webber said.

"No, you're going to Vietnam," the lieutenant said. "So get yourself and your crew into dress blues and get ready to meet the press."

Bernie was in a hurry all right, but it wasn't to get dressed. He got to a phone and quickly called Miriam.

Alex Larzelere, *The Coast Guard at War—Vietnam 1965–1975*
(Annapolis, Maryland: Naval Institute Press, 1997)

The deployment was explained at first as search and rescue off the coast of Vietnam, but that quickly morphed into search and destroy. The 82-foot cutters drew only a few feet of water. They were worked with the Swift Boats in riverine warfare. They patrolled, lead raids, evacuated trapped units, and served as fire support.

E-mail exchange between Bernard C. Webber and author, March 2008

But at home, Miriam and his children became the center of attention for those who opposed and supported the war. They felt incredible pressure to bear up, and it did not help that Bernie was not there. In those emotional times, you were a baby killer if you supported the war, or a peacenik hippie if you opposed it. Finally, the Webber family moved off the Cape and down to Florida, to escape the local notoriety.

E-mail exchange between Bernard C. Webber and author, March 2008

CHAPTER TWENTY-FIVE

The pinning ceremony involved mixing together the collar devices for new chief petty officers and seasoned chief petty officers. The intent was to underline traditions and symbolize the uninterrupted line of Coast Guard values and culture.

But one set of devices, worn smooth with time, was held aside and given to the newest chief petty officer. What's that about? Webster queried.

Those devices were worn by Bernie Webber, Downey said. They've been worn by nineteen new chief petty officers over the years. It lets the men know they are standing on the shoulders of heroes, Downey said.

Barbo, Webster, and Galluzzo, The Pendleton *Disaster*

Bibliography

Barbo, Theresa Mitchell, W. Russell Webster, and John Galluzo. *The Pendleton Disaster Off Cape Cod: The Greatest Small Boat Rescue in Coast Guard History.* Charleston, South Carolina: The History Press, 2007.

Beard, Barrett Thomas. *Wonderful Flying Machines: A History of U.S. Coast Guard Helicopters.* Annapolis, Maryland: Naval Institute Press, 1996.

Cahill, Capt. Richard A. *Disasters at Sea.* London: Century, 1990.

Hill, Donna. *David Atkins, Hero of Cape Cod. Wreck and Rescue Journal.* "They Had to Go Out" collection of stories. Avery Color Studios, Inc., Gwinn, Michigan, 2007.

Johns, Robert Erwin. *Guardians of the Sea.* Annapolis, Maryland: Naval Institute, 1987.

Noble, Dennis L. *Lifeboat Sailors.* Washington, D.C.: Brassey's, 2001.

———. *Rescued by the U.S. Coast Guard.* Annapolis, Maryland: Naval Institute Press, 2005.

Shields, Jerry. *The Invisible Billionaire Daniel Ludwig.* Boston: Houghton Mifflin Company, 1986.

Spyrou, Andrew G. *From T-2 to Supertanker: Development of the Oil Tanker, 1940–2000.* Lincoln, Nebraska: iUniverse, 2006.

Webber, Bernard C. *Chatham, "The Lifeboatmen:" A Narrative by a Seaman Recounting His Life in the Coast Guard at Chatham on the Southeast Corner of Cape Cod, Massach* (Orleans, Massachusetts: Lower Cape Publishing, 1985).

Wright, David, and David Zoby. *Fire on the Beach: Recovering the Lost Story of Richard Etheridge and the Pea Island Lifesavers.* New York: Scribner, 2000.

Index

About the Author

Robert R. Frump, a nationally recognized journalist, was for many years the maritime writer for *The Philadelphia Inquirer*. He and Tim Dwyer won the George Polk Award for their reporting on the wreck of the SS *Marine Electric*. He also was managing editor of Knight-Ridder's *The Journal of Commerce* and won the Loeb Award for National Business Reporting for a series on Delaware River ports. He is the author of two prior books, *Until the Sea Shall Free Them*, about the SS *Marine Electric*, and *Man-Eaters of Eden*, about human-animal conflict in Kruger National Park in South Africa. He and Suzanne Saxton-Frump, his wife, live in Summit, New Jersey.